ACKNOWLEDGMENTS

My husband BILL – I couldn't do what I do without your love and support. Thank you for loving me when I was fat and thin. You are the best husband a woman could ask for; you are my everything. Thank you for doing such an outstanding job with the food styling in this book.

My daughters KELLIE, RACHEL and JENNA – I am so proud of the women you are becoming. Your love and support fill my heart with joy and happiness.

My mum FAY - Thank you for being so proud of me and for all the support and love you give. My sister LEONIE who is so precious to me and is always there in good and bad times, you are a wonderful sister. LINDA my baby sister who is such a sweetie, love you lots and thank you LINDA for thinking of the title "SYMPLY TOO GOOD TO BE TRUE". Thank you to each one of you for believing in me and loving me unconditionally.

Management team – BMA SPEAKERS & CELEBRITIES BUREAU – I couldn't achieve all my goals without your support, guidance and expertise. Thank you Bebe, Stuart and team for believing in what I do and helping me to achieve my dreams. Ph: Bebe (07) 3854 1561.

Photographer SALLY – Your talent is second to none and I am grateful that you have been with me for every book. Thank you for making my books look so good; you are such a talent. Ph: Sally (07) 5474 9129.

Dietitians BILL SHRAPNEL, JANET FRANKLIN, ALAN BARCLAY & LISA COCHRANE – Thank you for your words of wisdom and support which I greatly appreciate. Your knowledge and expertise is outstanding.

Printer – THE INK SPOT PRINTERS. JOHN, CHRISTINE, IAN and TEAM. Thank you for doing an exceptional job. You are the best and I value your skills and support. Ph: (07) 5443 5431.

Graphics – CHILLI DESIGNS. Thank you Darren, Natalie and team for your expertise. Book 4 is amazing thanks to your talents. Ph: (07) 5437 7788

Myer, Maroochydore – To KAREN, DOT and TEAM. Nothing was too much trouble and I thank you for your help. All homeware products used in this book were provided courtesy of Myer. To contact your nearest Myer store please call 1800 811 611.

Distributors – NETWORK SERVICES – Thank you PHILLIP, ANDREW, JAMES, SHERRYL & DAVID - for your continued support. To date I have sold over 1 million books and without a doubt I know that I couldn't have achieved this without you by my side. Ph: Andrew (02) 92828702

Proof readers – SUE, VICKI, FIONA, LEETA, KATH and BMA team. Thank you so much for doing such a great job on the book. It was a real challenge and I appreciate the time and effort that it took to do what you did. A special thank you to Sue. Final editing by Bryan Ward. email: thewritestuffinoz@hotmail.com

Taste testers – JENNA, JAN, GEORGE, GEORGIA, VICKI, DIRK and SIMON. Thank you for your tastebuds and opinions; your dedication to eating was second to none and helped me create this outstanding cookbook. Also thanks to TARA for your help.

To my family and friends – I love you all and can't thank you enough for always being there in both the good and bad times. I am so grateful to have you all in my life.

To everyone who has helped, supported or owns one of my cookbooks I can't thank you enough for what you have helped me achieve. Without you I wouldn't be where I am today. If I have helped in anyway to improve your health or to give you enjoyment with cooking then I feel blessed.

Thank you everyone from the bottom of my healthy heart.

MW00906265

Contents

WELCOME BACK ONCE MORE TO MY WORLD OF TASTY LOW FAT COOKING.

I am thrilled to return with what I believe is an outstanding cookbook, "SYMPLY TOO GOOD TO BE TRUE 4". I am so proud of this new book filled with more wonderful recipes that I am sure you will enjoy. With 3 cookbooks that include such a vast array of choices, I thought when I started writing book 4 "what could I have possibly missed in the other 3 cookbooks?" I also wondered what people usually like but can't have because of the high fat content. Before I knew it, I was a woman on a mission; the recipes spilled out of me and the challenge in writing this new cookbook was one that I enjoyed immensely.

My goal with each new cookbook, is to improve on the book I wrote previously! I believe I have achieved this with book 4, and now offer you more recipes that you never thought could be made low fat. Any favourites that I may have missed in my other cookbooks can now be found in book 4, so you can continue enjoying what Mum or Gran used to make years ago without the guilt, and know that they have been adapted to a much healthier way of cooking. All my cookbooks not only have got low fat options, but are also encouraging many people into adapting a healthier way of living.

I listen to everyone who has offered me an opinion on what should be included in any new cookbook. This is one reason why I added a new section to this book titled "PARTY FOOD". You asked for it, and you got it! Everyone wants to know how to do party food without resorting to deep-fried, fatty pastries, and other high fat choices, so here it is folks - enjoy! I must admit, even I was surprised at how I was able to change some of our favourites in this new book. I feel blessed that I have been able to offer more unique recipes for you to enjoy and I hope you enjoy this book as much as the others. For me personally, I had a ball writing this book - I love it!

Over the years I have noticed everyone is getting more and more interested in what they are eating and what contents are in it. We are more educated on "what to eat" and "what not to eat" and our awareness about food is starting to show. For example, when I released book 1 back in late 1997 I listed five different subjects in the nutritional breakdown. Now, some 7 years later, book 4 has a total of 10 subjects in the nutritional breakdown,

making this book one of the most informative low fat cookbooks in Australia.

I applaud you for asking for more and more information and I am happy to add this information to my cookbooks for you whenever possible. I hope this information is of value to you and helps you understand what you are eating and gives you the confidence to know that when it comes to one of Annette Sym's recipes, you are making a healthier eating choice.

The nutritional information I am now offering in my cookbooks is - fats, saturated fats, fibre, protein, carbohydrates and sugars that are listed separately, plus sodium, kilojoules and calories and the glycemic index ratings.

You will also notice that I have added a few extras in book 4, such as information on my fantastic CD-Rom MENU PLANNER, that has helped so many people win the battle of the bulge (check out the testimonials page). Something I know you will find very handy is that I have also included a MASTER INDEX to help you find your favourite recipes from all my four cookbooks and a

The old Annette at 100 kilos and the healthy Annette at 65 kilos.

The adjustable teaspoon and tablespoon can be purchased from my website: www.symplytoogood.com.au or Phone 07 5445 1250

Measuring Cups and Spoons

In every recipe a metric measuring cup and spoon were used. For example the tablespoon I have used, equals 15 grams. If you were using a metal tablespoon be aware that it could measure from 20 to 30 grames a spoon. I didn't use a tea cup. When I say 1 cup of flour, I have used a 250ml measuring cup as shown.

section on oven temperatures and measurements to help avoid any confusion. I have also listed ingredients in order of use, to make cooking even easier.

Thank you to all of you who have one of my cookbooks. You have given me so much joy and happiness, knowing that you have valued my recipes and keep asking for more. I hope my new cookbook "SYMPLY TOO GOOD TO BE TRUE 4" will become one of your favourites. I wish you all a healthy and happy life, filled with all you wish for and more.

Finally I would like to dedicate this book to my beloved Grandmother Eva Parker who passed away when I was 9 years old. I know that if she were alive today she would have been the proudest grandmother in the world. Nan was a very big part of my life in those early years and I think of her every day. Miss you Nan.

ENJOY EVERY MOUTHFUL!

Measurements and Oven Temperatures

Liquid Measures

Metric		Imperial
5ml	(1 teaspoon)	⅛fl oz
10ml	(1 dessertspoon)	⅓fl oz
15ml	(1 tablespoon)	½fl oz
30ml		1fl oz
125ml	(½ cup)	4fl oz
150ml		5fl oz (¼pint)
250ml	(1 cup)	8fl oz
300ml		10fl oz (½pint)
500ml		16fl oz
600ml		20fl oz (1pint)
1000ml	(1 litre)	32fl oz (1¾pints)

Dry Measures

Metric	Imperial
15g	½oz
30g	1oz
125g	4oz (¼lb)
250g	8oz (½lb)
375g	12oz (¾lb)
500g	16oz (1lb)
750g	24oz (1½lb)
1kg	32oz (2lb)

All eggs used in the recipes are approx 60g

Oven Temperatures (guide only)

	°C (Celsius)	°F (Fahrenheit)	Gas Mark
Very Slow	120	250	1
Slow	150	300	2
Moderately Slow	160	325	3
Moderate	180	350	4
Moderately Hot	200	400	5
Hot	220	450	6
Very Hot	240	500	7

If not using a fan forced oven set temperature 10ºC higher than the temperature stated in my recipes. Also extend the cooking time for an extra 10-15 minutes. With baking check after 5 minutes. As every oven is different this is only a guide.

Freezing Tips

All recipes in all my cookbooks are suitable to be frozen but having said this, I would like to offer some tips on freezing:

1.   If cooking for 1 or 2 people you can either halve the ingredients in my recipes or freeze the remaining portion of the meals.

2.   If you make a dish that has a milky sauce, you should only freeze for 2-3 weeks, as the milk may curdle.

3.   Freezer burn occurs when moisture is lost or ice crystals evaporate from the surface of a product. To prevent it happening, package food in a heavyweight, moisture-resistant wrap or freezer containers that have good seals.

4.   Don't stack meat parcels on top of each other but lay them out flat in one layer instead of 4 layers of thicknesses. When freezing mince flatten out as this way it freezes and thaws quicker.

5.   Label food with the name of the dish and the date it was frozen and how many it serves.

6.   Baked goods such as cakes, scones, muffins and pikelets freeze really well, but freeze without icing.

Dietitian's Tips

Written by
Alan Barclay

B Sc; Grad Dip; APD

Research & Development Manager

Diabetes Australia-NSW

THE GLYCEMIC INDEX

Most foods that we eat are made up of a mix of the three main nutrients: carbohydrate, fat, and protein. Carbohydrate foods are one of the best sources of energy for our body, being the preferred fuel for our muscles and most of our organs. Foods high in carbohydrate include fruit, milk, yoghurt, breads, cereals, legumes (e.g. beans, lentils, chickpeas) and starchy vegetables like corn, potato, and sweet potato.

Of course, not all carbohydrate foods are the same: nearly all are digested and converted to glucose, but they do so at different rates - some slow, some fast. Once upon a time, carbohydrate foods were grouped according to how much sugar and starch (complex carbohydrate) they contained. Foods high in simple sugars include fruit, dairy foods, and table sugar, whereas foods high in starch include breads, cereals, legumes, and starchy vegetables. This system of classifying carbohydrates was based on the physical structure of the carbohydrate in the food. It was assumed that simple sugars were quickly absorbed into the blood while starches were slowly absorbed. Based on these assumptions, people were advised to eat mainly starches and to limit foods that were high in simple sugars.

In the 1980s, a new method of classifying carbohydrate foods, called the Glycemic Index, was developed. It proved once and for all that all sugars are not absorbed quickly into the blood and that not all starches are slowly absorbed.

So, what is the Glycemic Index or GI? The GI is a ranking of carbohydrates in food according to their effect on blood glucose (sugar) levels after eating. Foods with a low GI (less than 55) cause blood glucose levels to rise more slowly, over a longer period of time than high GI foods (70 or more). So low-GI foods are the best choices when trying to maintain constant energy levels, and when aiming to keep blood glucose levels lower for longer. High-GI foods, on the other hand, are useful during prolonged physical activity (longer

Food Groups	Examples
Breads	Wholegrain, multigrain, fruit loaf
Cereals	Pasta, noodles, etc... Basmati or Doongara rice breakfast cereals e.g. All-bran, Guardian, Komplete, Traditional Rolled Oats, etc...
Vegetables - starchy	Sweet potato, sweet corn
Legumes	All beans (except broad), lentils and chickpeas
Fruits	Orchard fruits: e.g. apple, orange, pear, peach, plum, and grapes.

than one hour) or for treating hypoglycaemia.

Not all carbohydrate foods eaten need to be low-GI, however. Authorities recommend that you try to eat at least one serve of low-GI carbohydrates at each meal, or base at least two meals each day on low-GI choices. The table above lists commonly eaten lower-GI foods:

Recipes in this book have their glycemic index ranked as either low, medium or high which I have calculated for Annette to help you maintain optimal energy and blood glucose levels.

Look for the Glycemic Index
Tested symbol when shopping

To help consumers use the GI more effectively, the University of Sydney, Diabetes Australia, and the Juvenile Diabetes Research Foundation joined forces and developed the Glycemic Index Symbol Program, which provides an easily recognised logo that consumers can trust for healthier food options:

The logo tells you

1. That a food has had its GI measured properly, at an approved GI testing facility

2. Meets the program's strict nutrition criteria.

3. A food is consistent with the dietary guidelines for Australians.

4. That its GI value is printed near the nutrition panel on the pack.

The nutrition criteria require foods to contain at least 10 grams of carbohydrate per serve, and must meet specified limits for

| **Total Fat, Sodium, Dietary Fibre, Calcium and Energy** |

For more information about the program visit our website: **www.gisymbol.com**

© &™ The University of Sydney

Written by
Janet Franklin

BMedSci (hons) MNutr/Diet APD

Metabolism & Obesity Services Royal Prince Alfred Hospital NSW

WHY AM I OVERWEIGHT?

Often people cannot understand why they are so overweight. Looking around your family, both immediate and extended, can give some insight into this question. Body shape and size seem to run in families. Usually you can identify someone else you look like; a parent, cousin, aunt, uncle or grandparent could have a similar body shape and size to your own. If there were a family pattern it would indicate a genetic predisposition to weight gain, meaning that you put weight on more easily than people who have a whole family of very lean people. However, this doesn't mean that you will always be that size, it just suggests that you may have to work harder at losing weight than others. Behavioural and environmental factors also play a role in weight. For instance, you may have had periods of overeating and/or inactivity that have lead to more weight gain than normal, or perhaps you have changed from using public transport to traveling by car, or from physical labour to a desk job.

Steps to success:

1. Do not starve yourself.

Being too restrictive or not eating for long periods can actually lead to eating too much for your body. Highly restrictive intakes can set up many feelings within us:

a) Feelings of extreme hunger often lead to eating more food than normal, and eating it more quickly. The food that is normally available at these times is high-energy, high-fat snack food. Eating these foods can sabotage the great work that you are trying to achieve.

b) Feelings of missing out, or being deprived. These feelings can make you want to break out of the restriction and eat. And you may start to ask questions like: "Why me? Why can I not eat whatever I want, whenever I want? Others can."

c) The body wants to seek food. This makes sense; if you were starving in the desert, you would not survive if you sat under a tree waiting for the food to come to you, you would need to go and seek the food. It is these same body responses that make you go and seek food when you are trying to limit intake. Therefore by being a little less restrictive you avoid these feelings, and at the same time, control your intake.

2. Eat regularly.

It can help you avoid thinking about food and severe hunger pangs, and allows you to continue to enjoy your food. Having 3 meals a day keeps your metabolism at a rate suitable for burning fat.

3. Eat foods high in fibre.

These will not only keep you regular and help prevent long-term disease, but will also add bulk to your food without adding any extra calories. That means that you can still feel that you are eating and becoming full, but not gain weight.

4. Re-assess what's on your plate.

Often the portions on your plate can give you a good indication of whether there is a particular food type you need to cut back on. Half of the food on your plate should be vegetables. Vegetables add fibre and bulk to your meal as well as providing all the vitamins and minerals your body needs. They are also low in calories so are unlikely to effect weight gain. One third of the food on your plate should be carbohydrate; this could include pasta, rice, potato, or bread. Carbohydrate is important as it provides the energy muscles need to function. However, too much carbohydrate can turn to fat if we are not active enough. The rest of the meal, which is about one quarter, is your protein source. This includes red meats, chicken, fish, tofu, cheese, nuts, legumes, lentils, or eggs. A piece of meat the size of your palm should be sufficient. Veal, turkey and white fish are often the leanest meats to eat.

5. Keep a diary.

Many people find keeping a diary an effective way to keep their weight under control. It lets you know when you have not eaten enough and when you have eaten too much to help you understand why your weight fluctuates and how to keep it in control. When you are writing down your food intake you are likely to be more conscious of what you are eating. All too often we have finished something before we have realised that we are eating it.

6. Eat slowly.

Enjoying your food helps you to be more satisfied, as well as giving you time to register your hunger and satiety signals. Make your meal place pleasant and sit down to eat, as this can add to the experience of eating, and thus the enjoyment of the food.

Written by
Bill Shrapnel

B App Sc, Grad Dip Nutr & Diet, MHP

FAT, CHOLESTEROL & HEART HEALTH

What is fat?

Fat is one of the three major components of food. The other two are carbohydrate and protein. All foods are combinations of fat, carbohydrate and protein.

Do I need to eat fat?

Yes. Everyone needs to eat some fat. Fat is a source of six essential nutrients for the body – vitamins A, D, E and K and the two essential fatty acids. A regular supply of all of these nutrients is needed to keep the body working properly.

Should I eat lots of fat?

No. A moderate amount will provide all the vitamins and essential fatty acids your body needs. More is not better. Fat is also a major fuel for the body – a concentrated source of kilojoules. Eating lots of fat will increase kilojoule intake and increase the chance of putting on weight.

Are some fats better than others?

Yes. Different fats have different effects on the level of cholesterol in the blood. Blood cholesterol is strongly linked to the risk of heart disease – the higher the cholesterol, the higher the risk. The problem fats are the saturated fats, which raise the level of cholesterol in the blood. Animal fats, for example those in dairy foods and fatty meats, are rich in saturated fats. Fats used to bake commercial biscuits, cakes and pastries contain plenty of saturated fats too. Takeaways and snack foods can also be a problem. Lowering the amount of saturated fats in daily meals is one of the most effective ways of lowering blood cholesterol.

Are there good fats?

Yes. Poly-unsaturated and mono-unsaturated fats are quite heart friendly. Most vegetable oils, and foods made from vegetable oils such as margarines and salad dressings, are rich in these 'good' fats. Monounsaturated & polyunsaturated fats do not raise blood cholesterol. In fact, the polyunsaturated fats have a cholesterol-lowering effect. Nuts, olives and avocados are rich in good fats too. Replacing some saturated fats with good fats will lower blood cholesterol.

Do the plant sterol margarines really lower cholesterol?

Yes. They are very effective. The plant sterols they contain are natural substances that block the absorption of cholesterol from the gut. As a result, cholesterol is swept out of the body each day and the level of cholesterol in the blood falls. The average fall in LDL-cholesterol is about 10 per cent. Plant sterol spreads start to work immediately and their full effect is evident within three weeks.

What dietary changes will lower blood cholesterol?

- Choose sunflower, canola or olive oils in cooking and salads

- Use a plant sterol spread or a good quality margarine instead of butter

- Include some nuts, olives and avocados in your meals

- Limit cream and cheese; choose low fat milk and yoghurt

- Limit fatty sausages and luncheon meats – choose lean meats and fish

- Limit biscuits, cakes and pastries – bake at home with margarine

- Go easy on the takeaways and snack foods.

Left: Lisa Cochrane
BSc. Grad Dip Diet.
MPH APD
Senior Dietitian
Diabetes Australia -
Victoria

> **Dietitian's Tip:**
> Look for these notes throughout the book for my tips & advice to assist people with diabetes.
> *Lisa Cochrane*

THIS COOKBOOK HAS BEEN ENDORSED BY DIABETES AUSTRALIA.

Diabetes Australia are happy to assist with any questions or concerns you may have. Ring on their toll free number **1300 136588**

DIABETES AUSTRALIA

Testimonials

My hubby Norm and I have been using your CD-Rom Menu Planner for 17 weeks now and am over the moon with the results. The food is yummy, easy to follow and cook. I am very pleased to say I have dropped 16 kilos and Norm 8 kilos. I have never felt better in years and would recommend your eating plan to anyone wanting to lose weight the happy way. In that 17 week period we also had a 4 week holiday touring, so it can be done if on your eating plan. Thank you Annette for changing our lifestyle.
Gail & Norm Vearing - Lake Albert NSW

Both my husband and myself send you our heartfelt thanks for your fantastic books. We now only use your cookbooks. With your recipes and a little exercise my husband has lost 30 kilos and I have lost 31 kilos. We both feel the fittest and healthiest we have in years. We thank you for all your hard work and the inspiration you have been to us and also to many other people. You are a truly great Australian.
Sue Kelly - Gaven Heights QLD

I felt I had to write and let you know how much your books have helped me lose 59 kg and counting. I cook up 3 or 4 different recipes from your books and put them in the freezer. I get home from work now and eat one of those meals, so much better than grabbing the first thing I lay my eyes on. With the help of your recipes I know I will reach my target weight. Thank you and well done on some great recipes. I look forward to your next book with great interest.
Caryl Linke - Valley View SA

I was lucky enough to attend one of your seminars. I say lucky because it changed my life forever. You are such an inspirational speaker, and I left that night knowing I was going to lose weight, get healthy and be the person I wanted to be. I proudly tell you that I'm now at my ideal weight, having lost 25 kilos and feel fantastic. Using your cookbooks and CD has taught me so much. Thank you.
Tracey Charters - Ipswich QLD

Annette, I can't begin to tell you what a change your recipe books have brought to our lives and just at the right time. My husband has cholesterol and high blood pressure problems and I've been battling a weight problem for years. Yo-yo dieting and all the rest. I was lamenting my problem to my friend Des in Darwin, and she told me to have a look at your site. I was so thrilled that I immediately ordered your first 3 books and haven't looked back since. My husband has lost 8kg and I've lost 10. We both feel so healthy and wow, there's no getting bored with all those recipes. I haven't seen any health recipe books in our bookstores here in South Africa that come anywhere near yours. My husband and I are both looking forward to recipe book No. 4. Your fan forever.
Brenda Greeff - Cape Town SOUTH AFRICA

I have been using your cookbooks as bibles for the past 10 months. My sons think I am the best cook in the world, and to top it off my husband has lost 15 kilos, I have lost 50 kilos, and my youngest son has lost 5 kilos. I can't thank you enough.
Rhonda Harris - Mackay QLD

Thank you Annette, your books have been my greatest inspiration to losing weight. I have been overweight from the age of 7. Over the years I just gradually got bigger. I had tried every diet and joined almost every club, only ever with short-term success; the diets were always so boring. Your recipes are

Gail before and after her weight loss of 40 kilos.

the tastiest I have had the pleasure to try, and so simple. I joined the Suncoast Slimmers Club as well to keep an eye on my success and kept a Food Diary. My first weigh-in was at 104kgs. I now weigh 64kgs and have lost 40kgs in 18 months, and feel truly wonderful. I've never been happier or more confident.
Gail Alford - Dicky Beach QLD

I can't speak highly enough of your books. My husband David was diagnosed with high cholesterol. As a marathon runner & a lover of desserts (every night) and cakes and biscuits, he was one unhappy chappie when I suggested he would have to give up these things. Then your books were suggested (a friend saw them on TV) and they have become our "bibles". I have a weight issue so it's been a two-fold battle and we're winning!! My husband's cholesterol has dropped so no medication, and I'm losing weight without feeling I'm on a diet. I recommend your books to everyone I meet. Thank you Annette from our entire family.
Debbie Mims - Carnegie VIC

Thank you for the new me. Christmas 1999 I weighed 110 kilos; a big smiley lady, but desperately unhappy inside. July 2001 I was diagnosed with type 2 diabetes. The hospital dietitian recommended your books and I have found them to be so helpful. The kilos just dropped off. My arthritic knees said thank you and in December 2001 I had lost a total of 35 kilos and have been so ever since. My diabetes is stable and no medication is needed. My favourite recipes are Mango Chicken, Banana Cake and Tiramisym – yum! I am 64 years of age and I thank you for changing my life.
Phyllis Turner - Campbelltown NSW

I was having chemotherapy for cancer. As I am overweight the doctors told me to go on a diet, but not to expect to lose weight whilst on the program. My sister put me onto your books and I haven't looked back. Even with chemo I have been able to lose 21 kilos in 6 months. Everyone was amazed. Your recipes are so nice why would anyone want to eat the high-fat way? I am determined to lose more weight. Thank you for your support.
Sharon Duxbury - Nanango QLD

Your recipes are excellent. Easy and quick to make, delicious and above all HEALTHY. They do us good, not only to reduce our weight but for diabetics too. It is so good to have books that do it all. I have my favourites that I make often, which the

children also enjoy even if they include vegies. Amazing when you consider how many children don't enjoy eating vegetables. I live in England and I have succeeded in buying all three books via your website.
Linda Patterson - Blyth. United Kingdom

Your cookbooks are a valuable resource of recipes to complement the nutritional education I give to my clients. Quick and simple, yet delicious and full of flavoursome meals, which adhere to today's nutritional guidelines suitable for the whole family. Congratulations Annette.
Selena Chan Accredited Practising Dietitian - Gold Coast Hospital - Robina Campus. QLD

A catch up from Cathy Chapman (testimonial in book 1): I have known Annette since 1998. We have remained in touch since our first meeting when she saw my story about my weight problems in Take 5 magazine. I have all of Annette's books. Out of all the diets I have tried, nothing has worked as much as eating less fat and eating healthy and tasty food. Up to this day I still use these books as a guide to low fat healthy eating. The books have worked for me. With the help of Annette's cookbooks I have been able to achieve a long-term solution to my weight problems. I have never had so much variety to eat as in her books. I recommend them always. I can't wait to see book 4.
Cathy Chapman - Reservoir VIC

I just wanted to let you know how absolutely delighted I am with your recipes books! Since using them I have lost weight and my clothes are getting too big for me. I have found your recipes easy, tasty and effortless. Your 'symple' way is liberating, as I know that what I eat is helping me lose weight. Sincere thanks for what you have been able to do for me.
Kim - Wagga NSW

I bought your cookbooks in February 04 and now only a few months later I am 24 kilos lighter. I'm not on a diet I have discovered a way to have my cake and eat it too! I love cooking now and my family is so much the better for it. I feel terrific, as I am not on a diet but have made more a lifestyle change.
Julie Hadley - Tomerong NSW

I was 95 kilos now I'm down to 54 kilos, a 41 kilo loss (almost another person). I'm now a size 8-10, and the best thing of all is that I can now tie a bow on my runners straight. Thanks to your wonderful books, I have never looked back.
Donna Job - Berwick VIC

I cannot put into words how grateful I am to you for allowing me to access your books in braille. It is as though you have given me back a part of my life and independence that was missing. Family and friends cannot believe the difference in my confidence levels, attitude and ability in the kitchen now. Mum thinks that it is wonderful because she now arrives home to a meal on the table, and no longer has to worry about getting meals ready after she arrives home (and I do not have to go hungry until she gets home). Once again Annette, my deepest thanks and immense gratitude for helping to open up (what was once an inaccessible part of my life) a world of healthy, delicious cooking, and the eating strategies for when I am eating out.
Sharron Hodges - Kippa-Ring, QLD

I came across your books by browsing through the newsagents. I bought a copy and told my girlfriend about them; she just had been diagnosed with high cholesterol, high blood pressure and diabetes. I wanted to lose some weight. We couldn't be happier. I have lost 23 kilos and my girlfriend has dropped from 2½ pills for her blood pressure to ½ a pill; her doctor is amazed and so is she. So dear Annette, thank you so much for such great books. Keep up the good work. Thanks from two skinnier, healthier and happier women.
Renate and Janelle - Hervey Bay QLD

I have battled all my life with weight gain, yoyo dieting, bulimia and emotional eating. I just couldn't find a weight loss program I could live with but with your wonderful cookbooks I have great tasting, nutritious meals plus treats like cakes, slices and desserts. I have lost 40 kilos and maintained this weight loss for some time. I can't believe the energy I have. I feel and look better and my self-confidence has greatly increased. I now help others to lose weight, and I always recommend your cookbooks they are the answer to my prayers. I am very grateful to you Annette for your wonderful books and for the warm and friendly help I always receive when I phone you. I realise you must be a very busy person but you always find the time to personally encourage and help me. I appreciate your kindness and thank you so much.
Annie Stocks - Beerwah QLD

Annie before and after her weight loss of 40 kilos.

Our listeners LOVE Annette!!! She set the Illawarra on fire when she visited personally and we were thrilled to bits when Annette agreed to be a weekly guest on our breakfast show. Annette's health tips, menu ideas and her books are extremely popular. One listener has given up her lifetime membership with a diet club and swears by Annette's books for getting weight off, keeping it off and still enjoying eating! So glad book number 4 is here; we've been drooling with anticipation!!!!
Phebe Irwin and Dave Gorr, The Big Breakfast, Wave FM - Wollongong NSW

KEEPING MOTIVATED

Statistics say, 95% of people who lose weight regain the weight within 5 years. If we are to change these figures, we need to focus less on losing weight and instead look at ways to become a healthy person for life. It took me about 20 months to lose 35 kilos, and to be honest there were times I felt like giving up. Seven weeks into the program the novelty had started to fade and hunger took over. I remember saying to myself: "well if people don't like me as I am, then that's their problem", but I wasn't being honest with myself. I knew this wasn't about other people and what they thought, but it was about me and not wanting to be fat anymore. The other time I wasn't being honest with myself was ten kilos from goal weight when I became complacent and lost motivation. I felt great and I think I just rested on my laurels. What I did to overcome this complacency was a bit strange, but worked and can I suggest to anyone struggling with their weight loss to give this a go. I found a picture in a magazine of a girl who was slim and wearing jeans. I really wanted to be able to wear jeans, as I hadn't had a pair for many years. I found a photo of myself, cut out my face and stuck it over the picture of the slim girl wearing jeans. Instantly I had a positive visual to focus on, and it made me feel I wanted to keep going and lose those last remaining kilos. I wrote under the picture "JUST DO IT ANNETTE" and on another piece of paper I put 10 strikes. As I lost each kilo I crossed one out. As you know, I did reach my goal weight and all these years later I am here trying to help others to do the same. We all have good and bad moments in life and when losing weight we will have our ups and downs, but with the right attitude, you can achieve anything! Please don't ever give up on yourself, and stay positive by telling yourself if Annette can do it so can I. If I had given up I wouldn't have my several

pairs of jeans that I love to wear and a life filled with so much joy and abundant health. Take responsibility for your health and well-being and do whatever it takes to create the life that you deserve.

Annette at the North Shore Heart Research Foundation Diet and Excercise Forum 2004.

"I remember how these shorts just fitted me back when I weighed 100 kilos and now being able to fit into one leg shows what you can achieve."

OBESITY IN CHILDREN

They say that 1 in 3 children are carrying excess weight and Aussie kids are more overweight than ever before in history. As I was an overweight child I can understand both sides of the story. The problem with childhood obesity is due to overeating, bad food choices, and inactivity. I know from my own personal experience how it feels to be picked on at school, to be unable to run as fast as the other kids and not wear the clothes other girls wear. If you have a

Annette - "a chubby child"

child who has a weight problem here are a few tips:

1.   Parents are the providers, nurturers and mentors so lead by example. Children mirror their parents so take control of not only what you cook for your child, but also what's in the pantry and fridge. By making healthy choices for meals etc. you can help turn an unhealthy, unhappy child into a healthy happy child. It's not fun being an overweight adult, but for a child it can leave emotional scars that stay for life.

2.   Involve children in sport and becoming more active Limit the amount of time spent in front of the television and computer. The lack of activity in a child's day could be one of the main reasons why they are carrying excess weight.

3.   Unless the child is obese, never put them on a diet without medical advice. Offer them lots of healthy choices, and as they grow their weight will balance out. Set realistic goals that they can sustain. Involve the child in making decisions that may benefit them now and in their adult life. In their early years habits are created that can be taken into adulthood, encourage healthy choices so they have good health throughout their lives.

4.   Takeaways are very high in fat, for example, a meal from a well-known hamburger joint can be as much as 80gms of fat. Everything in moderation is the way to go with children and adults. Don't make take away food an everyday occurrence, keep as an occasional treat.

5.   The ideal snack should be low in fat, high in fibre and low in sugar and salt. The best snack of all is fresh fruit. Canned fruit that has no added sugar, low-jouled jellies, yoghurts, rice crackers or my low fat baking recipes to name just a few. For a great after school snack offer a bowl of high fibre cereal, skim milk and some chopped up fruit, which should fill them up until dinner time.

6.   It is not recommended to give skim milk to children under 5 years of age. Full cream milk has around 10grams of fat per glass as opposed to skim milk at 0.2grams of fat. Both have the same nutrients, the only difference is fat content.

7.   All children need a wide variety of food and nutrients from all food groups.

8.   Children have very little willpower and if food is in the cupboard, like biscuits and chips, they will eat it even if they know they shouldn't. Make your house a 'safe zone'. Buy only healthy food, so that if they are hungry they have only healthy choices to eat.

9.   If your child is overweight don't think they can lose weight on their own - they need your help, support, discipline and unconditional love. If your child is obese then please consult with your doctor or a dietitian.

10.   Above all never, ever tell a child or teenager that they are fat, even if you are joking.

ANNETTE'S TAKEAWAY MAKEOVERS

Most takeaways are both high in fat and low in fibre. Not ideal choices if you want to have a healthy diet. The words healthy and takeaway just don't seem to go together, but I am taking on the challenge - to makeover the deep fryer mayhem of takeaway meals. Everything in moderation is the key to healthy living, just don't make high fat takeaway meals a part of your weekly eating regime. They should be eaten only occasionally. Here are ways to reduce the fat count in take away meals:

1.　　Chinese or Asian restaurants really know how to do a great stir-fry. Full of vegetables, they are a great choice but there are a few things that you can do to make them even better. Don't like seeing oodles of fat sitting on the top of your stir-fry then next time you order, do what I do and tell them you want no oil used when they cook your dishes. Their woks are normally oiled well so it won't affect the dish. Flavours will be better and it will certainly help in the fat count. Avoid anything that is deep-fried, and where possible ask for steamed options. Have boiled rice instead of fried, and forget prawn crackers. If you have meat in your dish then forget ordering cashews or almonds as well; even though they are good for you they consist of just too much fat. Choose one or the other.

2.　　Australians love a good old-fashioned hamburger. My makeover is to have hamburgers plain with no butter on the bun. Ask for heaps of salad and forget ordering cheese, egg and bacon. With at least 6gms of fat for a slice of cheese or an egg, you don't need it.

3.　　I am concerned with what goes into some takeaway meals and how hygienic some places are. When in doubt, don't eat from any eateries you are not confident handle food appropriately or you can see the place is not clean.

4.　　Subway offers a few low fat choices but avoid having cheese and mayo as extras. Don't' go for a full sub a half a sub is big enough.

5.　　Pizza is a popular takeaway choice but can be high in fat. If you can limit yourself to 2 pieces it isn't too bad preferably with the thin crust. Toppings should include more vegetables and less fatty meats, and ask for less cheese. Have a big bowl of salad as well.

6.　　Fish and chips are a bit of a worry as they are deep fried. Fish is good for you and low in fat, but once deep fried it changes everything. Some shops offer the option of grilling your fish, which is a better choice. The best advice I can give you on chips is that thin chips are higher in fat, than thick chips. If you are concerned with cholesterol or want a low saturated diet, check that the fat used is either vegetable or sunflower oil, as you should avoid beef/pork fat where possible.

7.　　Seafood cooked the right way can be a slimmer's friend. Avoid having high fat sauces such as cocktail sauce; the better alternative sauce is my recipe in book 1. Keep seafood as natural as possible and remember, fish has the added value of omega 3s.

8.　　Deep fried chicken meals are both high in fat and low in fibre. Not recommended to have on a regular basis; keep as an occasional treat.

9.　　Salads, such as coleslaw and potato salad can be high in fat, due to the dressings used. Use my recipes where possible.

10.　　Snack size kebabs are good, but don't add extras such as cheese and high fat sauces. Even though tahini, avocado and hommus are a healthy choice they can be high in fat, so add sparingly.

PUT THE SALT SHAKER AWAY

It is important to monitor how much salt (sodium) is consumed in ones diet. Because of this, I have included the sodium information in this cookbook, to help not only people sensitive to sodium, but also for people with heart and cholesterol problems and people with diabetes.

A low sodium diet is beneficial to all of us as we are consuming far too much salt. Limiting the amount of salt in your diet, you can reduce fluid retention and also help lower blood pressure. If you suffer any of the abovementioned conditions, it is recommended you not only try to stay in your healthy weight range but you should also eat a well balanced, healthy diet that is low in saturated fats, high in fibre, low in salt and includes moderate amounts of carbohydrates and proteins. Even if you don't actually put salt in your cooking or on your food, you would be amazed at how much salt is in some foods, such as soft drinks, bread, pre-prepared foods, dry soup mixes and canned vegetables and let's not forget preserved ham, bacon, sausages and salamis, which are all high in salt.

There is more salt in cornflakes than in a packet of light chips, the salt is processed into the cornflakes so tastebuds don't notice the salt as much. Whereas chips are coated with salt so tastebuds get the salt hit straight away. This could explain why most people put sugar on many cereals. Choosing salt reduced products where available will help reduce the high sodium counts in a recipe. You will find many reduced salt or no added salt products in supermarkets and they taste great.

It is recommended to have no more than 2400 mg of sodium per day. Most sodium consumed in our diet is from table salt (sodium chloride) so instead of shaking salt onto your food try adding herbs to enhance taste. Re-training your tastebuds doesn't take as long as you might think. Yes, at first food does taste different without salt, but once you get used to it you will notice the flavours in food much more. Drinking at least 2 litres of water each day will help flush out toxins and assist with fluid retention as well. My final suggestion would be to throw out your saltshaker.

Spicy Potato Wedges

SERVES: 4

1 kilo potatoes

5 teaspoons reduced salt taco seasoning (Old El Paso®)

3 teaspoons Moroccan seasoning

cooking spray

DIRECTIONS

Preheat oven 230ºC fan forced.

Wash potatoes leaving skin on. Cut each potato in quarters. Cut each quarter into thick slices on an angle to get the potato wedge shape. Par boil potato in microwave in a little water for 10 to 12 minutes or until slices are half cooked. Drain well. Place seasonings and potato wedges in a large plastic freezer bag; shake together until wedges are evenly coated with seasoning. Generously coat a flat baking tray with cooking spray; spread wedges over tray. Coat wedges again with cooking spray. Bake 25-30 minutes or until potatoes are cooked.

Serve with Symple Sour Cream (Book 3) and sweet chilli sauce or salsa.

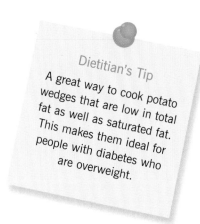

Dietitian's Tip
A great way to cook potato wedges that are low in total fat as well as saturated fat. This makes them ideal for people with diabetes who are overweight.

Pea and Ham Soup

SERVES: 10

1⅓ cups (250g) green split peas

1⅓ cups (250g) yellow split peas

2 cups carrots diced

1 onion diced

400g lean ham steaks diced

4 litres water

pepper to taste

DIRECTIONS

Soak peas in water as instructed on packet. Leave overnight. Drain and rinse well. Place all the ingredients into a boiler, stir together, bring to boil. Reduce to a slow boil for 2 hours; stir occasionally. Mash with a potato masher. Add pepper to taste.

Dietitian's Tip
Have this soup with multigrain bread for lunch or dinner. The meal is low in fat, high in fibre and the glycemic index is low making it an ideal choice for people with diabetes.

Nutritional Information

PER SERVE		
FAT	TOTAL	0.5g
	SATURATED	0g
FIBRE		5.3g
PROTEIN		6.2g
CARBS		34.3g
SUGAR		1.6g
SODIUM		232mg
KILOJOULES		719(cals 171)
GI RATING		High

Nutritional Information

PER SERVE		
FAT	TOTAL	3.5g
	SATURATED	1.0g
FIBRE		6.5g
PROTEIN		17.8g
CARBS		27.0g
SUGAR		3.9g
SODIUM		453mg
KILOJOULES		876(cals 208)
GI RATING		Low

Warm Chicken Salad with Mango Dressing

SERVES: 6

DRESSING: 1 x 400g can mango slices
1 teaspoon soy sauce
¼ teaspoon fish sauce
2 teaspoons sweet chilli sauce
SALAD: 1 lettuce
1 punnet cherry tomatoes
24 slices cucumber
½ large capsicum thinly sliced
1 small Spanish onion thinly sliced
CHICKEN: 2 teaspoons Creole seasoning
1 teaspoon salt reduced chicken-style stock powder (Massel®)
2 teaspoons dried onion flakes
500g raw chicken fillets
cooking spray

DIRECTIONS

To make dressing: Drain mango slices, reserve juice for dressing. Dice ¼ of the mangoes, leave to one side. Puree remaining mango slices with ¼ cup of the reserved juice. In a small mixing bowl add mango puree, soy, fish and sweet chilli sauces. Add diced mango, combine well. Leave to one side. **To make salad:** Wash and prepare salad ingredients and divide onto six dinner plates or bowls. Leave to one side. **To cook chicken:** Place Creole seasoning, stock powder and onion flakes into a medium sized plastic freezer bag. Add chicken fillets and coat well with seasonings. Generously coat a non-stick frypan with cooking spray, fry chicken fillets until cooked. Place fillets on top of salad then pour dressing over each serve.

Nutritional Information

PER SERVE	CHICKEN	RUMP
FAT TOTAL	3.2g	3.6g
SATURATED	0.8g	1.4g
FIBRE	3.4g	3.4g
PROTEIN	30.6g	31.6g
CARBS	14.7g	14.7g
SUGAR	12.5g	12.5g
SODIUM	337mg	331mg
KILOJOULES	887(cals 211)	918(cals 218)
GI RATING	Low	Low

Thai Carrot and Coconut Soup

SERVES: 8

cooking spray
1 kilo carrots sliced
1½ cups onion diced
2 teaspoons red curry paste (in jar)
1 teaspoon crushed garlic (in jar)
1 tablespoon salt reduced vegetable stock powder (Massel®)
1½ litres water
1 tablespoon soy sauce
1 teaspoon fish sauce
1 x 375ml can evaporated light milk
1 teaspoon imitation coconut essence
pepper to taste

Dietitian's Tip
A clever use of coconut essence and evaporated milk to give the flavour of coconut milk without the saturated fat.

DIRECTIONS

Coat a boiler with cooking spray, sauté carrots, onions and red curry paste for 3 minutes. Add all other ingredients except the milk and coconut essence. Bring soup to boil, lower heat and simmer 45 minutes. Add milk and coconut essence. Once boiled puree soup using either a food processor or Bamix®. Add pepper to taste.

Nutritional Information

PER SERVE	
FAT TOTAL	1.0g
SATURATED	0.5g
FIBRE	4.0g
PROTEIN	5.4g
CARBS	13.1g
SUGAR	12.7g
SODIUM	302mg
KILOJOULES	352(cals 84)
GI RATING	Low

Indian Beans with Chapatti Bread

SERVES: 6

BEAN MIX

1 x 420g can kidney beans

1 x 400g can borlotti beans

1 x 400g can cannellini beans

cooking spray

1 cup onion diced

¾ cup green capsicum diced

1 teaspoon crushed garlic (in jar)

1 x 415g can no added salt chopped tomatoes

1 x 400g can salt reduced tomato soup

2 teaspoons salt reduced vegetable stock powder (Massel®)

⅛ teaspoon chilli powder or to taste

2 teaspoons curry powder

CHAPATTI BREAD

1¼ cups plain flour

1 teaspoon baking powder

½ teaspoon crushed garlic (in jar)

1 teaspoon virgin olive oil

1 teaspoon salt reduced vegetable stock powder (Massel®)

½ cup water

TOPPING

¾ cup grated 25% reduced fat tasty cheese

Dietitian's Tip

A spicy low GI meal that will keep you feeling full and satisfied for hours.

DIRECTIONS

To make bread: In a large mixing bowl sift flour and baking powder. Add garlic, oil, stock powder and water to bowl and combine well. On a well-floured surface knead dough until smooth. Divide into 6 small balls. Cover balls with a tea towel and leave to rest for 1 hour (so the bread isn't tough). Once rested, on a well-floured surface roll out each ball until very thin, using a rolling pin. Coat a large non-stick frypan with cooking spray and fry each sheet for 15 seconds each side. Place cooked sheets on a tea towel, keep covered until required (this will keep the bread soft).

To make bean mix: Drain and wash all beans together. Coat a non-stick frypan with cooking spray, sauté onion, capsicum and garlic for 2 minutes. Add remaining ingredients. Bring to boil and slow boil 5 minutes.

To make topping: Place ⅙ of bean mixture in centre of each Chapatti bread sheet and roll up. Place on a baking tray and sprinkle cheese on top. Place under griller until cheese has melted.

VARIATIONS: OMIT CHAPATTI BREAD AND CHEESE AND SERVE BEANS ON THEIR OWN OR OVER POTATOES, RICE, PASTA OR ON TOAST.

Nutritional Information

PER SERVE		Beans/Chapatti	Beans Only	Chap/Bread Only
FAT	TOTAL	5.0g	0.9g	1.1g
	SATURATED	2.1g	0.1g	0.2g
FIBRE		10.1g	8.9g	1.1g
PROTEIN		15.9g	9.2g	3.2g
CARBS		47.0g	26.0g	21.0g
SUGAR		8.4g	8.4g	0g
SODIUM		474mg	382mg	2mg
KILOJOULES		1260(cals 300)	636(cals 151)	453(cals 108)
GI RATING		Low	Low	Low

Pizza Pasta Bake

SERVES: 6

2 cups dried penne pasta

cooking spray

1 teaspoon crushed garlic (in jar)

1 cup green capsicum cut into strips

1 small onion sliced

2 cups mushrooms sliced

1 cup (125g) 97% fat free thick sliced ham (KR®) cut into strips

1 x 415g can no added salt crushed tomatoes

1 x 420g can salt reduced tomato soup

2 tablespoons no added salt tomato paste

1 teaspoon dried oregano

1 teaspoon dried basil

2 tablespoons grated parmesan cheese

1¼ cups 25% reduced fat grated tasty cheese

DIRECTIONS

Preheat oven 180°C fan forced. Follow cooking instructions on pasta packet, leave to one side. Coat a large non-stick frypan with cooking spray, sauté garlic, capsicum and onion for 2 minutes. Add mushrooms and cook 2 minutes. Place all remaining ingredients into pan except for pasta and tasty cheese. Combine all ingredients well. Once boiled simmer for 3 minutes. Fold pasta and ½ cup tasty cheese into mixture. Pour mixture into a lasagne dish, level out then sprinkle remaining ¾ cup tasty cheese over top. Bake 30-35 minutes uncovered.

VARIATION: VEGETARIAN PIZZA PASTA BAKE, OMIT HAM AND REPLACE WITH 1 CUP SLICED CELERY.

Dietitian's Tip

This recipe contains vegetables, cereals, dairy and protein. Just add a fruit for dessert and it would be a complete meal.

Nutritional Information

PER SERVE		PIZZA	VEGETARIAN
FAT	TOTAL	7.0g	6.5g
	SATURATED	3.9g	3.7g
FIBRE		2.9g	3.3g
PROTEIN		16.8g	13.5g
CARBS		33.2g	33.5g
SUGAR		7.3g	7.4g
SODIUM		515mg	305mg
KILOJOULES		1110(cals 264)	1038(cals 247)
GI RATING		Low	Low

Chicken and Sweet Corn Soup

SERVES: 10

1 litre salt-reduced chicken stock liquid (Campbell's®)

1½ litres water

1 tablespoon salt reduced chicken-style stock powder (Massel®)

500g skinless chicken breast

½ cup shallots sliced

2 cups frozen corn kernels

2 x 420g cans creamed corn

3 tablespoons soy sauce 43% less salt

1 egg white

pepper to taste

Dietitian's Tip
This is a great choice for people wanting a tasty soup without it being high in sodium (salt). Ideal for those with high blood pressure.

DIRECTIONS

Place stock liquid, water and stock powder in boiler. Once boiled, add whole chicken breasts. Cook 10 minutes then remove chicken. Either shred or dice chicken then return to pot with shallots, corn kernels, creamed corn and soy sauce. Bring to boil, then reduce to slow boil. Cook a further 10 minutes. Whisk in beaten egg white. Add pepper to taste.

Tomato and Vegetable Soup

SERVES: 8

2 x 400g cans brown lentils

cooking spray

1 cup onion diced

1 teaspoon crushed garlic (in jar)

2 cups carrots diced

2 cups celery diced

3 litres water

2 x 415g cans no added salt chopped tomatoes

1 x 410g can tomato puree

1 tablespoon fresh basil finely chopped

1½ tablespoons salt reduced vegetable stock powder (Massel®)

1 tablespoon curry powder

pepper to taste

DIRECTIONS

Drain and wash canned lentils and leave to one side. Coat a large boiler with cooking spray, sauté onion, garlic, carrots and celery for 2 minutes. Add all remaining ingredients. Slow boil for 45 minutes, stir occasionally. Pepper to taste.

Dietitian's Tip
This is an ideal food choice for people who have a history of high blood pressure and diabetes.

Nutritional Information

PER SERVE		
FAT	TOTAL	1.8g
	SATURATED	0.9g
FIBRE		2.4g
PROTEIN		15.4g
CARBS		14.5g
SUGAR		4.4g
SODIUM		584mg
KILOJOULES		573(cals 136)
GI RATING		Low

Nutritional Information

PER SERVE		
FAT	TOTAL	0.5g
	SATURATED	0g
FIBRE		4.9g
PROTEIN		5.5g
CARBS		14.0g
SUGAR		7.7g
SODIUM		411mg
KILOJOULES		352(cals 84)
GI RATING		Low

Sundried Tomato Bread

MAKES: 15 SLICES

20g semi sundried tomatoes
1½ (22g) tablespoons Flora Light® margarine
2 teaspoons skim milk
1 teaspoon grated parmesan cheese
1 French bread stick (170g)

DIRECTIONS

Very finely chop sundried tomatoes. In a small mixing bowl beat margarine for 30 seconds using an electric beater. Slowly add milk (about ½ teaspoon at a time), until blended. Add sundried tomatoes and parmesan cheese and combine well. Cut bread stick into 15 slices, spread sundried spread over the top of each slice. Place under griller until golden brown. Serve as a starter or to accompany a meal.

VARIATION: CHEESY SUNDRIED BREAD. MAKE AS DIRECTED ABOVE THEN SPRINKLE ½ CUP 25% REDUCED FAT GRATED TASTY CHEESE OVER TOP BEFORE GRILLING. GRILL UNTIL CHEESE HAS MELTED.

Dietitian's Tip
This could be eaten as a snack instead of crisps or potato chips. This is a much healthier option as it is both low in fat and salt.

Penne Pasta in Creamy Bacon Sauce

SERVES: 4

3 cups dried penne pasta
cooking spray
¾ cup onion or shallots diced
1 teaspoon crushed garlic (in jar)
¾ cup bacon short cuts diced
1 x 375ml can evaporated light milk
¾ cup skim milk
1 tablespoon grated parmesan cheese
1 sachet Garden Harvest creamy mushroom cup-a-soup (Continental®)
1 teaspoon salt reduced chicken-style stock powder (Massel®)
1 tablespoon cornflour
pepper to taste

DIRECTIONS

Follow cooking instructions on pasta packet, leave to one side. Coat a large saucepan with cooking spray, sauté onion, garlic and bacon until browned. In a small bowl place both milks, parmesan cheese, soup sachet, stock powder, cornflour and whisk together. Add to saucepan, stir continuously until boiled. Fold pasta gently through sauce until heated through. Pepper to taste.

Dietitian's Tip
The creamy taste in this recipe is not due to high fat sauces but evaporated light milk. You may like to use this product instead of cream in other recipes.

Nutritional Information

PER SERVE	SUNDRIED	CHEESE
FAT TOTAL	1.4g	2.2g
SATURATED	0.3g	0.8g
FIBRE	0.4g	0.4g
PROTEIN	1.2g	2.2g
CARBS	6.2g	6.2g
SUGAR	0.7g	0.7g
SODIUM	88mg	112mg
KILOJOULES	177(cals 42)	223(cals 53)
GI RATING	High	High

Nutritional Information

PER SERVE	
FAT TOTAL	8.1g
SATURATED	3.7g
FIBRE	3.0g
PROTEIN	23.4g
CARBS	67.9g
SUGAR	14.8g
SODIUM	494mg
KILOJOULES	1852(cals 441)
GI RATING	Low

Antipasto Pasta

SERVES: 6

300g dried pasta

350g red capsicum

350g zucchini

350g eggplant

cooking spray

1 large onion

2 teaspoons garlic (in jar)

2 cups mushrooms quartered

½ cup dry white wine

1 x 425g can chopped tomatoes

2 tablespoons no added salt tomato paste

1 tablespoon fresh basil chopped

½ cup (75g) semi sundried tomatoes cut in half

¼ cup (25g) Spanish olives sliced

¼ cup grated parmesan cheese

1 teaspoon salt reduced chicken-style stock powder (Massel®)

DIRECTIONS

Follow cooking instructions on pasta packet, leave to one side. Cut capsicum into large slices lengthways removing core and seeds. Slice each zucchini into 3 slices lengthways. Cut eggplant into 1½cm slices. Coat a flat baking tray with cooking spray, place capsicum, zucchini and eggplant slices on tray then coat with cooking spray. Place under griller and cook until browned on both sides (capsicum needs to be grilled until outside skin blisters). Once cooled remove skin from capsicum. Cut grilled vegetables into large slices, leave to one side. Slice onion in quarters then cut into thick slices. Coat a non-stick frypan with cooking spray, sauté onion for 2 min. Add mushrooms, cook 2 min. Place white wine in pan and cook 30 seconds then add canned tomatoes, tomato paste, basil, sundried tomatoes, olives, parmesan cheese and stock powder, stir ingredients well. Fold grilled vegetables and pasta into sauce until well combined.

VARIATION: OMIT PASTA OR FOR A WHEAT FREE ALTERNATIVE USE RICE PASTA MACARONI (BUONTEMPO®) SOLD IN SUPERMARKETS IN THE HEALTH FOOD SECTION.

Dietitian's Tip

This contains lots of tomatoes making it high in vitamin C. This vitamin helps with wound healing and absorbing iron into the body.

Nutritional Information

PER SERVE		WITH PASTA	W/OUT PASTA
FAT	TOTAL	6.1g	5.7g
	SATURATED	1.7g	1.6g
FIBRE		8.5g	7.3g
PROTEIN		14.8g	10.8g
CARBS		41.4g	17.6g
SUGAR		16.5g	16.5g
SODIUM		452mg	450mg
KILOJOULES		1262(cals 300)	775(cals 185)
GI RATING		Low	Low

Marinated Vegetable Kebabs

SERVES: 8 AS A SIDE DISH

MARINADE

½ cup dry white wine

2 tablespoons no added salt tomato paste

¼ cup Thai chilli jam paste (in jar)

1 teaspoon crushed garlic (in jar)

1 teaspoon crushed ginger (in jar)

KEBAB

1 large (125g) onion

1 large (130g) red capsicum

2 medium (275g) zucchinis

16 cherry tomatoes

16 medium sized mushrooms

DIRECTIONS

Soak Kebab sticks in water before use to avoid burning. In a medium sized bowl combine all marinade ingredients. Leave to one side. Peel and cut ends off onion. Cut in quarters. Cut each piece in half again (8 pieces). Divide each piece of onion in two (16 pieces). Cut 4 large slices off capsicum, remove core then cut each piece into quarters. Cut ends off zucchinis then cut each zucchini into 8 slices (16 slices). With each skewer place 1 piece of onion, capsicum, zucchini, cherry tomato and mushroom, repeat again. Repeat this process with remaining skewers. Place the vegetable kebabs into a large shallow plastic container that has a lid, pour marinade over vegetables. Place lid on top and refrigerate. Turn kebabs occasionally. Marinate vegetables overnight if possible, or for at least 4 hours. When ready to cook, remove kebabs from marinade mix and either barbecue or grill, turning so all sides cook through. Pour marinade over vegetables while cooking.

VARIATION: REPLACE VEGETABLES WITH OTHER VEGETABLES E.G. EGGPLANT, CELERY, YELLOW SQUASH, CARROT OR PUMPKIN.

Dietitian's Tip

Five serves of vegetables a day are recommended for good health. Having a couple of these kebabs would definitely move you towards this guideline.

Beans 'N' Bacon

SERVES: 6 AS A SIDE DISH

500g fresh green beans

cooking spray

½ teaspoon crushed garlic (in jar)

½ cup onion finely diced

½ cup bacon short cuts diced

2 tablespoons no added salt tomato paste

pepper to taste

DIRECTIONS

Trim ends off beans. Microwave in a little water until beans are cooked to your liking. Drain.

Coat a non-stick frypan with cooking spray, sauté garlic, onion and bacon until cooked. Add tomato paste and beans, toss until beans are coated with sauce.

Dietitian's Tip

Microwave the beans for a short time to retain the water-soluble vitamins.

Nutritional Information

PER KEBAB		
FAT	TOTAL	1.0g
	SATURATED	0.2g
FIBRE		1.8g
PROTEIN		2.4g
CARBS		5.0g
SUGAR		4.4g
SODIUM		121mg
KILOJOULES		209(cals 50)
GI RATING	*Not available due to the low carb content*	

Nutritional Information

PER SERVE		
FAT	TOTAL	0.8g
	SATURATED	0.2g
FIBRE		2.4g
PROTEIN		4.5g
CARBS		2.9g
SUGAR		1.9g
SODIUM		176mg
KILOJOULES		160(cals 38)
GI RATING	*Not available due to the low carb content*	

Kashmir Rice

SERVES: 4 AS A SIDE DISH

¾ cup raw Basmati rice

1 teaspoon turmeric

¼ teaspoon salt

¼ cup sultanas

1 small onion

cooking spray

¼ cup slivered almond

½ teaspoon crushed garlic (in jar)

½ teaspoon crushed ginger (in jar)

¼ teaspoon garam masala

¼ teaspoon cardamom

½ teaspoon Indian curry powder

½ teaspoon chicken stock powder

Dietitian's Tip
Using Basmati rice ensures there is ample low glycemic index carbohydrates.

DIRECTIONS

Bring a medium sized saucepan ¾ filled with water to boil. Once boiling add rice, turmeric and salt, stir well. Reduce to a slow boil. In the last couple of minutes before rice is cooked add sultanas. Once rice is cooked (approximately 12 minutes). Turn rice into a colander and rinse well. Leave to drain. Peel onion and cut in quarters, then cut into thin slices. Coat a small non-stick frypan with cooking spray, sauté onion and almonds until browned. Add garlic and ginger and cook for 30 seconds. Place garam masala, cardamon, curry powder and chicken stock powder into pan and cook for 30 seconds. Place rice into a large bowl and fold in onion mix.

Nutritional Information

PER SERVE		
FAT	TOTAL	3.9g
	SATURATED	0.3g
FIBRE		1.6g
PROTEIN		4.5g
CARBS		40.0g
SUGAR		8.2g
SODIUM		120mg
KILOJOULES		888(cals 211)
GI RATING		Medium

Vegetarian Burger

SERVES: 6

cooking spray

1 teaspoon crushed garlic (in jar)

1 small onion finely diced

½ cup red capsicum finely diced

½ cup frozen peas

½ cup frozen corn kernels

1 x 420g can kidney beans drained

1 x 400g can brown lentils drained

1 cup dried breadcrumbs

1 egg white

1 teaspoon salt reduced vegetable stock powder (Massel®)

2 tablespoons no added salt tomato paste

1 sachet Garden Harvest creamy mushroom cup-a-soup (Continental®)

pepper to taste

DIRECTIONS

Coat a non-stick frypan with cooking spray, sauté garlic, onion, capsicum, peas and corn until cooked, leave to one side. Place kidney beans and lentils into a food processor and process until finely chopped. Add all other ingredients including sautéed vegetables. Blend well. Pepper to taste. Shape into 6 large patties. Generously coat a non-stick frypan with cooking spray, heat pan and cook burgers until both sides have browned.

Nutritional Information

PER BURGER ONLY		
FAT	TOTAL	1.2g
	SATURATED	0.2g
FIBRE		5.9g
PROTEIN		8.5g
CARBS		24.5g
SUGAR		3.9g
SODIUM		379mg
KILOJOULES		604(cals 144)
GI RATING		Low

Annette's Pasta Salad

SERVES: 8 AS A SIDE DISH

2 cups dried macaroni pasta
1 whole egg
½ cup 97% fat-free mayonnaise (Kraft®)
2 tablespoons grated parmesan cheese
cooking spray
½ teaspoon crushed garlic (in jar)
¾ cup short cut bacon diced
½ cup frozen corn kernels
3 shallots sliced
1 cup mushrooms sliced

DIRECTIONS

Follow cooking instructions on pasta packet, leave to one side. Bring a small saucepan ¾ filled with water to boil, once boiling place egg in and boil for 4 minutes. Rinse egg under cold water for a few minutes to cool slightly. Shell egg, leave to one side. Using blender or a Bamix® combine egg with mayonnaise and parmesan cheese until smooth. Coat a small non-stick frypan with cooking spray, sauté garlic and bacon until browned. Microwave corn in a little water for 2 minutes, drain. In a large bowl combine pasta, mayonnaise dressing, bacon mix, corn, shallots and mushrooms folding well.

Dietitian's Tip

This pasta salad has lots of low glycemic index carbohydrates.

Nutritional Information

PER SERVE		
FAT	TOTAL	4.0g
	SATURATED	1.6g
FIBRE		1.8g
PROTEIN		7.8g
CARBS		29.8g
SUGAR		5.0g
SODIUM		302mg
KILOJOULES		791(cals 188)
GI RATING		Low

Rosemary Potatoes

SERVES: 6 AS A SIDE DISH

1 kilo potatoes
cooking spray
3 teaspoons dried rosemary

DIRECTIONS

Preheat oven 230°C fan forced.

Peel and wash potatoes then dice into medium sized pieces. Par boil in microwave in a little water for 5 to 6 minutes. Drain well. Generously coat a flat baking tray with cooking spray, spread out diced potatoes and spray with cooking spray. Sprinkle rosemary over potatoes. Bake 30-35 minutes or until potatoes are browned, turning once.

Dietitian's Tip

A great way to cook low fat and low salt potatoes instead of fried chips. Ideal for people with diabetes.

Nutritional Information

PER SERVE		
FAT	TOTAL	0.7g
	SATURATED	0.4g
FIBRE		3.4g
PROTEIN		4.5g
CARBS		28.0g
SUGAR		7.8g
SODIUM		107mg
KILOJOULES		577(cals 137)
GI RATING		High

Carrot and Spinach Slice

SERVES: 6

1 bunch silverbeet/spinach

2 whole eggs

3 egg whites

1 x 35g packet salt reduced French onion soup (Continental®)

1 teaspoon crushed garlic (in jar)

2 tablespoons grated parmesan cheese

½ cup 25% reduced fat grated tasty cheese

3 cups carrot grated

½ cup onion diced

¾ cup self raising flour

pepper to taste

cooking spray

extra ½ cup 25% reduced fat grated tasty cheese

DIRECTIONS

Preheat oven 180°C fan forced. Wash silverbeet then remove white stalks. (An easy way to do this is to hold the stalk in one hand and with the other hand pull away the green leaf). Cut silverbeet leaves into thin strips. Microwave in a little water for 3 minutes. Drain really well by pushing out as much water as possible from silverbeet and leave to one side. In a large mixing bowl beat eggs and whites well. Add dry soup mix, garlic, parmesan cheese, ½ cup tasty cheese and combine well. Add in grated carrots, diced onion and spinach and mix. Stir in flour until combined well. Coat a quiche dish with cooking spray then spread mixture into dish. Sprinkle extra ⅓ cup tasty cheese over top. Bake 45 minutes or until browned and firm in centre.

VARIATION: FOR A QUICKER VERSION REPLACE SILVERBEET WITH 2 x 250g PACKETS FROZEN CHOPPED SPINACH. DEFROST AND SQUEEZE AS MUCH WATER OUT AS POSSIBLE FROM SPINACH BEFORE USING.

Dietitian's Tip
Carrots are rich in vitamin A, is essential for normal vision and growth.

Nutritional Information

PER SERVE

FAT	TOTAL	6.8g
	SATURATED	3.5g
FIBRE		4.1g
PROTEIN		12.7g
CARBS		16.8g
SUGAR		4.1g
SODIUM		464mg
KILOJOULES		749(cals 178)
GI RATING		Medium

Vegelicious

SERVES: 4 AS A SIDE DISH

- 1 bunch fresh asparagus
- cooking spray
- 1 teaspoon crushed garlic (in jar)
- ½ cup onion diced
- 4 cups (300g) mushrooms quartered
- ¼ teaspoon turmeric
- ¼ teaspoon cumin
- ¼ teaspoon dried coriander
- ¼ teaspoon paprika
- 1 punnet cherry tomatoes

DIRECTIONS

Cut 3cm off end of each asparagus spear and throw away. Cut spears into 3cm pieces. Coat a non-stick frypan with cooking spray, sauté garlic, onion and asparagus for 2 minutes. Add mushrooms and cook for 2 minutes. Add spices and cook 1 minute. Add tomatoes and cook 1 to 2 minutes or until heated through.

Dietitian's Tip

Mushrooms contain vitamin B12 responsible for blood cell development.

Deluxe Potato Salad

SERVES: 8 AS A SIDE DISH

- 750g potatoes
- 750g orange sweet potatoes
- ½ cup Spanish onion sliced or ½ cup shallots finely sliced
- 2 tablespoons mint finely chopped
- ½ cup extra-light sour cream
- ¼ cup caesar 99% fat-free dressing Kraft®
- pepper to taste

DIRECTIONS

Peel both potatoes and cut into cubes (about 1½ to 2cm). Microwave in a little water for 15 to 20 minutes or until just cooked through. Once cooked, turn into a colander and run cold water over potato for a few minutes. Leave to drain. Cut onion in quarters and slice finely. Place potato and onion into a large mixing bowl. In a small mixing bowl combine mint, sour cream and caesar dressing. Add dressing to potato and fold gently until combined. Add pepper to taste.

Dietitian's Tip

The sweet potato lowers the glycemic index of this salad.

Nutritional Information

PER SERVE

FAT	TOTAL	0.5g
	SATURATED	0g
FIBRE		4.5g
PROTEIN		5.2g
CARBS		4.6g
SUGAR		3.0g
SODIUM		16mg
KILOJOULES		186(cals 44)
GI RATING	*Not available due to the low carb content*	

Nutritional Information

PER SERVE

FAT	TOTAL	0.7g
	SATURATED	0.4g
FIBRE		3.4g
PROTEIN		4.5g
CARBS		28.0g
SUGAR		7.8g
SODIUM		107mg
KILOJOULES		577(cals 137)
GI RATING		Medium

Seafood

Honey Prawn Stir-Fry

SERVES: 4

- 1 tablespoon sesame seeds
- 1½ cups carrots
- 1½ cups snow peas
- 1 cup broccoli
- ½ cup shallots
- 400g peeled raw prawns
- cooking spray
- ½ teaspoon crushed garlic (in jar)
- ½ teaspoon crushed ginger (in jar)
- 1 cup water
- 1 teaspoon reduced salt chicken-style stock powder (Massel®)
- 1 teaspoon soy sauce 43% less salt
- 2 tablespoons cornflour
- ⅓ cup honey

DIRECTIONS

Toast sesame seeds under griller (be careful as they can burn quickly). When toasted leave to one side. Peel carrots then cut in half lengthways then slice at an angle. Cut snow peas in half on an angle. Slice shallots. Cut broccoli into small florets. To butterfly the raw peeled prawns (this makes the prawn more tender), using a sharp knife run the blade down the back of the prawns being careful not to cut all the way through, scrape out the vein. Rinse prawns. Coat a wok or non-stick frypan with cooking spray, sauté garlic and ginger for 30 seconds, add prawns and cook 2 to 4 minutes (depending on size) until just cooked. Remove prawns from wok, leave to one side. Re-heat wok, add ¼ cup of water, carrots and broccoli, cook 2 minutes then add shallots and snow peas, cook for 2 minutes. Add stock powder and soy sauce. Combine cornflour with remaining water then add to wok. Add honey, sesame seeds and prawns, combine well.

VARIATIONS: REPLACE PRAWNS WITH EITHER 500g BONELESS FISH FILLETS, BUTTERFLY PORK STEAKS OR SKINLESS CHICKEN BREASTS, ALL VARIATIONS CUT INTO STRIPS.

Dietitian's Tip

This dish is very low in fat and high in flavour, protein, vitamins and minerals making it a healthy recipe for people with diabetes.

Creamy Tuna Bake

SERVES: 6

- 1½ cups dried macaroni pasta
- 2 x 425g cans tuna in spring water drained
- cooking spray
- 1 teaspoon crushed garlic (in jar)
- 2 cups mushrooms sliced
- ½ cup shallots or onion sliced
- 1 cup frozen corn kernels
- 1 x 310g can creamed corn
- 2 teaspoons salt reduced chicken-style stock powder (Massel®)
- 2 x 30g sachets 4 cheese sauce (Continental®)
- 1½ cups boiling water
- ½ cup 25% reduced fat grated tasty cheese

DIRECTIONS

Preheat oven 180°C fan forced. Cook pasta as instructed on packet, leave to one side. Drain tuna and roughly break up, leave to one side. Coat a large non-stick frypan with cooking spray, sauté garlic and mushrooms, cook 2 minutes. Add tuna, shallots, corn kernels, creamed corn and stock powder, combine. In a small bowl combine 4 cheese sauce with boiled water until blended. Add cheese sauce to pan, fold together. Add pasta and stir well. Pour into a casserole dish. Sprinkle cheese over top and bake 30 minutes or until cheese has melted and browned on top.

VARIATIONS: FOR A QUICKER VERSION, OMIT BAKING IN OVEN AND INSTEAD PLACE LASAGNE DISH UNDER GRILLER TO BROWN CHEESE TOP OR REPLACE TUNA WITH 500g SKINLESS CHICKEN BREASTS DICED. COAT FRYPAN WITH COOKING SPRAY AND COOK CHICKEN.

Nutritional Information

PER SERVE		PRAWN	FISH	PORK	CHICKEN
FAT	TOTAL	1.7g	1.2g	2.4g	4.0g
	SATURATED	0.2g	0.1g	0.5g	0.9g
FIBRE		3.4g	3.4g	3.4g	3.4g
PROTEIN		23.8g	36.0g	33.8g	31.5g
CARBS		31.9g	31.9g	31.9g	31.9g
SUGAR		27.7g	27.7g	27.7g	27.7g
SODIUM		440mg	202mg	155mg	158mg
KILOJOULES		986(cals 235)	1176(cals 280)	1180(cals 281)	1201(cals 286)
GI RATING		Low	Low	Low	Low

Nutritional Information

PER SERVE		TUNA	CHICKEN
FAT	TOTAL	6.2g	5.5g
	SATURATED	2.7g	2.2g
FIBRE		4.2g	4.2g
PROTEIN		34.1g	28.2g
CARBS		37.1g	37.1g
SUGAR		3.7g	3.7g
SODIUM		375mg	339mg
KILOJOULES		1437(cals 342)	1310(cals 312)
GI RATING		Low	Low

Fish Mornay

SERVES: 6

750g boneless fish fillets

cooking spray

½ cup onion diced

½ teaspoon crushed garlic (in jar)

2 tablespoons cornflour

1 x 375ml can evaporated light milk

½ cup 25% reduced fat grated tasty cheese

3 tablespoons grated parmesan cheese

pepper to taste

DIRECTIONS

Cut fish into bite sized pieces. Coat a large non-stick frypan with cooking spray, sauté onion and garlic for 1 minute. Add fish to pan and cook 3 minutes. Combine cornflour with evaporated milk, add to pan, stir well. Add tasty cheese and parmesan cheese and combine. Pepper to taste.

VARIATIONS: REPLACE FISH WITH EITHER RAW SCALLOPS, FRESH SALMON FILLETS OR 600g SKINLESS CHICKEN BREASTS.

Dietitian's Tip
The National Heart Foundation recommends that we have three serves of fish per week.

Scallops Provencale

SERVES: 6

cooking spray

½ cup onion diced

1 teaspoon crushed garlic (in jar)

750g raw scallops

½ cup dry white wine

1 x 415g can crushed tomatoes

2 tablespoons no added salt tomato paste

¼ teaspoon dried basil

¼ teaspoon dried thyme

¼ teaspoon dried oregano

2 tablespoons cornflour

¼ cup water

pepper to taste

Dietitian's Tip
A nutrient rich low fat, low salt and high-protein recipe.

DIRECTIONS

Coat a large non-stick frypan with cooking spray, sauté onion and garlic for 1 minute. Add scallops to pan and cook 1 minute. Add wine, crushed tomatoes, tomato paste and all herbs to pan. Combine cornflour with water then stir into mixture. Pepper to taste.

VARIATIONS: REPLACE SCALLOPS WITH EITHER 600g PEELED RAW PRAWNS, 600g BONELESS FISH FILLETS DICED OR 600g SKINLESS CHICKEN BREASTS DICED.

Nutritional Information

PER SERVE		FISH	SCALLOPS	SALMON	CHICKEN
FAT	TOTAL	5.5g	5.5g	8.9g	6.9g
	SATURATED	3.1g	3.2g	3.0g	3.6g
FIBRE		0.2g	0.2g	0.2g	0.2g
PROTEIN		31.6g	24.2g	34.6g	32.3g
CARBS		9.9g	10.6g	9.9g	9.9g
SUGAR		7.6g	7.7g	7.6g	7.6g
SODIUM		297mg	390mg	186mg	241mg
KILOJOULES		907(cals 216)	795(cals 189)	1110(cals 264)	972(cals 231)
GI RATING		Low	Low	Low	Low

Nutritional Information

PER SERVE		SCALLOPS	PRAWNS	FISH	CHICKEN
FAT	TOTAL	1.1g	0.8g	0.9g	2.5g
	SATURATED	0.3g	0.1g	0.1g	0.6g
FIBRE		1.0g	1.0g	1.0g	1.0g
PROTEIN		15.5g	21.5g	18.5g	23.6g
CARBS		6.6g	5.9g	5.9g	5.9g
SUGAR		3.2g	3.1g	3.1g	3.1g
SODIUM		256mg	402mg	141mg	107mg
KILOJOULES		463(cals 110)	554(cals 132)	506(cals 120)	652(cals 155)
GI RATING		Low	Low	Low	Low

Gourmet Seafood Lasagne

SERVES: 6

2 x 30g sachets 4 cheese sauce (Continental®)

2 cups boiling water

3 tablespoons cornflour

1½ cups skim milk

1 x 425g can crushed tomatoes

½ teaspoon dried basil

1 teaspoon crushed garlic (in jar)

cooking spray

250g boneless fish fillets diced

250g raw peeled prawns

250g fresh salmon fillet diced

150g raw calamari rings

150g raw scallops

½ cup shallots sliced

2 tablespoons parmesan cheese

9 dried lasagne sheets

¾ cup 25% reduced fat grated tasty cheese

DIRECTIONS

Preheat oven 180°C fan forced.

In a small bowl combine 4 cheese sauce with boiling water, stir in well, leave to one side. Combine cornflour with skim milk, leave to one side. In another small bowl combine crushed tomatoes, basil and garlic, leave to one side. Coat a large non-stick frypan with cooking spray, sauté fish, prawns, salmon, calamari and scallops until just cooked (about 3 to 4 minutes). Add shallots to seafood. Pour cheese sauce into pan and stir well, then add parmesan cheese and skim milk. Bring to boil, stir continuously, leave to one side. Coat a lasagne dish with cooking spray, spread 3 lasagne sheets over base. Pour half of the seafood mixture over lasagne sheets then top with 3 more lasagne sheets. Pour remaining seafood mix over then cover with the last 3 lasagne sheets. Top with tomato mix and then sprinkle with grated cheese. Cover with foil. Bake 45 minutes. Remove foil and cook a further 15 minutes.

Dietitian's Tip

Seafood has Vitamin B1, thiamin, this is required for muscle strength, memory and appetite.

Nutritional Information

PER SERVE		
FAT	TOTAL	8.4g
	SATURATED	3.5g
FIBRE		1.6g
PROTEIN		41.5g
CARBS		29.8g
SUGAR		6.4g
SODIUM		525mg
KILOJOULES		1525(cals 363)
GI RATING		Low

Fish with Smoked Salmon and Cream Cheese Sauce

SERVES: 4

100g smoked salmon (Royal Tasmanian®)
cooking spray
¼ cup shallots sliced
½ teaspoon crushed garlic (in jar)
1½ tablespoons cornflour
1 x 375ml can evaporated light milk
10 capers chopped (in jar)
¼ packet x 250g Light Philadelphia®
cream cheese
½ teaspoon fish sauce
pepper to taste
4 x 125g boneless fish fillets

DIRECTIONS

Cut salmon into bite sized pieces, leave to one side. Coat a medium sized saucepan with cooking spray, sauté shallots and garlic for 30 seconds. Combine cornflour with evaporated milk, add to pan, stir continuously until boiled. Reduce heat, add salmon, capers, cream cheese and fish sauce, stir until cheese has melted. Pepper to taste. Lower heat and keep hot while fish is cooking. Generously coat a large non-stick frypan with cooking spray, fry fish fillets for 2 to 3 minutes each side or until just cooked and browned (turn only once to avoid drying fish out). Place fish on serving plates and pour sauce over top.

VARIATIONS: REPLACE FISH WITH SKINLESS CHICKEN BREASTS OR LEAN RUMP STEAKS.

Nutritional Information

PER SERVE		FISH	CHICKEN	RUMP
FAT	TOTAL	8.7g	10.7g	11.1g
	SATURATED	2.0g	2.6g	3.2g
FIBRE		0.2g	0.2g	0.2g
PROTEIN		31.5g	37.9g	38.9g
CARBS		14.4g	14.4g	14.4g
SUGAR		11.7g	11.7g	11.7g
SODIUM		539mg	496mg	490mg
KILOJOULES		1187(cals 283)	1370(cals 326)	1401(cals 334)
GI RATING		Low	Low	Low

Red Salmon Potato Pie

SERVES: 4

750g potatoes peeled
2 tablespoons skim milk
cooking spray
½ cup onion diced
3 tablespoons cornflour
½ teaspoon crushed garlic (in jar)
1 x 375ml can evaporated light milk
½ cup skim milk
1 x 415g can red salmon drained
1 tablespoon fresh parsley finely chopped
2 tablespoons grated parmesan cheese
pepper to taste
¼ cup 25% reduced fat grated tasty cheese

Dietitian's Tip
Salmon contains essential fatty acids, essential for people with diabetes.

DIRECTIONS

Dice potatoes then microwave in a little water until cooked. Drain well, add 2 tablespoons skim milk and mash using a potato masher until smooth, leave to one side. Coat a medium sized saucepan with cooking spray, sauté onion and garlic for 2 minutes. Combine cornflour with evaporated milk and ½ cup skim milk and add to saucepan, bring to boil. Roughly break up salmon then add to saucepan with parsley and parmesan cheese, mix well. Pepper to taste. Pour mixture into a small lasagne or casserole dish then top with mashed potato. Place spoonfuls of mashed potato over top of salmon mix (using a fork to help spread potato evenly over the top). Sprinkle grated cheese over potato then place under griller until browned on top.

VARIATIONS: REPLACE WITH EITHER CANNED PINK SALMON DRAINED OR TUNA IN SPRING WATER DRAINED.

Nutritional Information

PER SERVE		RED	PINK	TUNA
FAT	TOTAL	11.7g	9.5g	6.4g
	SATURATED	4.0g	4.3g	3.5g
FIBRE		4.1g	4.1g	4.1g
PROTEIN		33.9g	34.4g	35.9g
CARBS		44.1g	44.1g	44.1g
SUGAR		15.2g	14.4g	14.4g
SODIUM		627mg	670mg	275mg
KILOJOULES		1748(cals 416)	1682(cals 400)	1606(cals 382)
GI RATING		Medium	Medium	Medium

Spicy Thai Fish

SERVES: 4

500g boneless fish fillets

1 onion

cooking spray

1 teaspoon crushed garlic (in jar)

1 teaspoon crushed ginger (in jar)

1 cup capsicum diced

1 cup celery sliced

1.cup carrot sliced

1 cup snow peas cut in half

1 x 415g can no added salt crushed tomatoes

2 tablespoons no added salt tomato paste

1 tablespoon fresh coriander chopped

2 teaspoons lemon grass (in jar)

4 teaspoons red curry paste (in jar)

1 teaspoon salt reduced vegetable stock powder (Massel®)

½ teaspoon chilli powder (optional)

2 teaspoons fish sauce

1 tablespoon cornflour

⅛ cup water

Dietitian's Tip

A very low fat interesting recipe. The basmati rice will increase the carbohydrate content. For most people half to three quarters of a cup of cooked Basmati rice is sufficient.

DIRECTIONS

Use a firm fleshed fish in this recipe to avoid fish crumbling e.g. flake. Cut fish into bite sized pieces. Peel and cut onion in half then slice. Generously coat a non-stick frypan or wok with cooking spray, sauté garlic and ginger for 30 seconds, add fish pieces to pan and toss gently together until fish is just cooked (about 2 to 3 minutes). Remove fish from pan, leave to one side. Re-spray pan with cooking spray and sauté onion, capsicum, celery and carrots for 3 minutes. Add snow peas and cook 2 minutes, stir frequently to avoid vegetables burning. Place tomatoes, tomato paste, coriander, lemon grass, red curry paste, stock powder, chilli powder and fish sauce into pan and combine. Combine cornflour into water and add to pan, stir until thickened. Gently fold fish through sauce (to avoid it breaking up). Serve with Basmati rice.

VARIATIONS: REPLACE FISH WITH EITHER SKINLESS CHICKEN BREASTS CUT INTO STRIPS OR 400g TOFU DICED.

Nutritional Information

PER SERVE		FISH	CHICKEN	TOFU
FAT	TOTAL	1.0g	3.8g	6.9g
	SATURATED	0.1g	0.9g	0.1g
FIBRE		3.8g	3.8g	3.8g
PROTEIN		36.2g	31.7g	13.5g
CARBS		14.0g	14.0g	18.0g
SUGAR		9.1g	9.1g	10.1g
SODIUM		474mg	431mg	368mg
KILOJOULES		890 (cals 212)	915(cals 218)	683(cals 163)
GI RATING		Low	Low	Low

Chicken Kiev

SERVES: 4

FILLING

1½ tablespoons (25g) Flora Light® margarine

2 teaspoons crushed garlic (in jar)

1 teaspoon parsley finely chopped

1 teaspoon skim milk

CHICKEN

4 x 125g skinless chicken breasts

8 toothpicks

1 egg white

2 tablespoons skim milk

⅓ cup dried breadcrumbs

cooking spray

DIRECTIONS

Preheat oven 180ºC fan forced.

In a small mixing bowl beat margarine, garlic and parsley for 30 seconds. Slowly add milk a little at a time until blended. Leave to one side. Using a mallet flatten chicken breasts. Spoon a quarter of margarine mixture onto centre of each chicken piece. Lift edges of chicken and then roll breast up over filling tightly, making sure filling is well sealed inside the chicken breast roll. Secure chicken with a couple of toothpicks in each breast. On a dinner plate beat egg white and milk together. Pour breadcrumbs onto another plate. Coat chicken in egg mix then roll in breadcrumbs until well coated. Coat a baking tray with cooking spray, place chicken on tray and coat with cooking spray. Bake 20-25 minutes or until chicken is cooked through.

Dietitian's Tip
The taste of the deep-fried traditional recipe without the fat. Ideal for weight conscious people with diabetes.

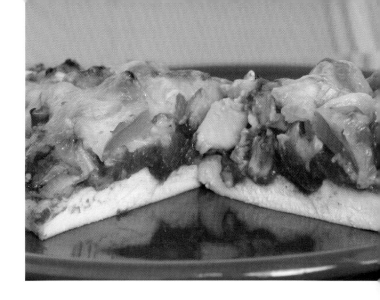

Acapulco Chicken

SERVES: 4

4 x 125g skinless chicken breasts

cooking spray

2 tablespoons salt reduced taco seasoning (Old El Paso®)

3 tablespoons no added salt tomato paste

½ cup onion diced

⅛ teaspoon chilli powder (optional)

½ cup green capsicum diced

½ cup tomatoes diced

½ large (60g) avocado diced

½ cup 25% reduced fat grated tasty cheese

DIRECTIONS

Preheat oven 180ºC fan forced. Using a mallet flatten chicken breast. Coat a baking tray with cooking spray then place chicken on tray. In a small bowl combine taco seasoning and tomato paste. Spread an even amount over each chicken breast. In a medium sized mixing bowl place onion, chilli powder, capsicum, tomato and avocado and combine. Spread mixture evenly over each chicken breast, top with cheese. Bake 20-25 minutes or until chicken has cooked through and cheese has melted and browned.

VARIATIONS: REPLACE CHICKEN WITH EITHER LEAN RUMP STEAK, BONELESS FISH FILLETS OR 400g TOFU.

Dietitian's Tip
Avocado is high in monounsaturated fat. Ideal for heart health in people with diabetes.

Nutritional Information

PER SERVE	
FAT TOTAL	6.3g
SATURATED	1.4g
FIBRE	0.6g
PROTEIN	30.7g
CARBS	5.8g
SUGAR	1.1g
SODIUM	163mg
KILOJOULES	852(cals 203)
GI RATING	*Not available due to the low carb content*

Nutritional Information

PER SERVE	CHICKEN	STEAK	FISH	TOFU
FAT TOTAL	9.7g	10.0g	7.7g	12.8g
SATURATED	3.4g	4.0g	2.8g	2.6g
FIBRE	1.5g	1.5g	1.5g	1.5g
PROTEIN	33.5g	34.5g	27.2g	15.3g
CARBS	4.3g	4.3g	4.3g	8.3g
SUGAR	3.4g	3.4g	3.4g	4.4g
SODIUM	413mg	407mg	456mg	351mg
KILOJOULES	1009(cals 240)	1041(cals 248)	827(cals 197)	778(cals 185)
GI RATING	*Not available due to the low carb content*			

Butter Chicken

SERVES: 6

800g skinless chicken breasts
cooking spray
1 medium sized onion diced
1 teaspoon crushed garlic (in jar)
½ teaspoon crushed ginger (in jar)
1 teaspoon cinnamon
1 teaspoon turmeric
1 teaspoon dried coriander
2 teaspoons paprika
½ teaspoon cumin
⅛ teaspoon chilli powder
2 teaspoons chicken stock powder
4 tablespoons no added salt tomato paste
1 tablespoon cornflour
1 x 375ml can evaporated light milk

Dietitian's Tip
This recipe does not contain butter but uses cooking oil. This lowers the amount of saturated fat and kilojoules making it an ideal food choice.

DIRECTIONS

Cut chicken into bite sized pieces. Coat a large non-stick frypan or wok with cooking spray, sauté chicken, onion, garlic and ginger until chicken pieces are nearly cooked. Add all the spices and stock powder. Combine with chicken for 1 minute. Add tomato paste and fold through chicken. Blend cornflour with milk then add to pan, stir continuously mixing well until boiled.

VARIATIONS: REPLACE CHICKEN WITH EITHER LEAN RUMP STEAK, BUTTERFLY PORK STEAK OR 600g TOFU.

Nutritional Information

PER SERVE		CHICKEN	RUMP	PORK	TOFU
FAT	TOTAL	4.5g	4.9g	2.8g	7.4g
	SATURATED	1.6g	2.2g	1.2g	0.8g
FIBRE		0.4g	0.4g	0.4g	0.4g
PROTEIN		36.5g	37.5g	38.9g	16.3g
CARBS		12.3g	12.3g	12.3g	16.3g
SUGARS		9.1g	9.1g	9.1g	10.1g
SODIUM		386mg	380mg	482m	17mg
KILOJOULES		991(cals 236)	1024(cals 244)	968(cals 230)	721(cals 172)
GI RATING		*Not available due to the low carb content*			

Lemon Chicken

SERVES: 4

cooking spray
4 x 125g skinless chicken breasts
¼ cup lemon juice
1 teaspoon lemon rind finely grated
1 teaspoon chicken stock powder
½ cup loosely packed brown sugar
2 tablespoons honey
¼ teaspoon soy sauce
2 teaspoons cornflour
¼ cup water

DIRECTIONS

Coat a large non-stick frypan with cooking spray, fry chicken until cooked through turning once. Remove from pan, leave to one side. Place all other ingredients into pan except water and cornflour. Stir ingredients well until boiling. Combine cornflour with water and add to pan. Bring back to boil, stir continuously. Cut chicken into large slices then return chicken to pan and re-heat, coating with sauce.

Dietitian's Tip
Have the lemon chicken with Basmati rice to make it a nutritious low-glycemic index meal.

VARIATION: REPLACE CHICKEN WITH BONELESS FISH FILLETS.

Nutritional Information

PER SERVE		CHICKEN	RUMP
FAT	TOTAL	7.3g	7.7g
	SATURATED	2.3g	2.9g
FIBRE		1.9g	1.9g
PROTEIN		34.0g	35.0g
CARBS		11.1g	11.1g
SUGAR		5.4g	5.4g
SODIUM		425mg	419mg
KILOJOULES		1122(cals 267)	1153(cals 275)
GI RATING		Medium	Medium

Tuscan Chicken with Pasta

SERVES: 4

1½ cups dried penne pasta

500g skinless chicken breasts

1 bunch fresh asparagus

cooking spray

2 teaspoons crushed garlic (in jar)

1 cup zucchini sliced

1 cup capsicum sliced

1 cup onion diced

2 x 425g cans crushed tomatoes

2 tablespoons no added salt tomato paste

2 teaspoons salt reduced chicken-style stock powder (Massel®)

¾ teaspoon dried mixed herbs

2 tablespoons grated parmesan cheese

DIRECTIONS

Cook pasta as instructed on pasta packet, leave to one side. Cut chicken into bite sized pieces. Cut 3cms off ends of asparagus spears and throw ends away. Cut spears into 2cm pieces. Coat a non-stick frypan with cooking spray, sauté garlic for 15 seconds, add diced chicken and cook for 3 minutes. Place asparagus, zucchini, capsicum and onion in with chicken and cook 2 minutes. Add all remaining ingredients to pan and bring to boil. Reduce heat and cook on slow boil for 5 minutes. Stir in cooked pasta.

VARIATIONS: REPLACE CHICKEN WITH EITHER 500g LEAN RUMP STEAK, 500g BUTTERFLY PORK STEAKS, 400g PEELED RAW PRAWNS, 500g BONELESS FISH FILLETS OR 400g TOFU.

Dietitian's Tip
Through removing the skin from the chicken the amount of fat is reduced making it a suitable recipe for people with diabetes.

Nutritional Information

PER SERVE	CHICKEN	RUMP	PORK	PRAWN	FISH	TOFU
FAT TOTAL	5.2g	5.6g	3.6g	2.6g	3.2g	8.3g
SATURATED	1.6g	2.2g	1.2g	1.0g	1.0g	0.9g
FIBRE	6.3g	6.3g	6.3g	6.3g	6.3g	6.3g
PROTEIN	38.0g	39.0g	40.3g	30.3g	31.6g	19.8g
CARBS	35.9g	35.9g	35.0g	35.9g	35.9g	39.9g
SUGAR	10.7g	10.7g	10.7g	10.7g	10.7g	11.7g
SODIUM	273mg	267mg	370mg	555mg	316mg	211mg
KILOJOULES	1540(cals 367)	1571(cals 374)	1519(cals 362)	1325(cals 315)	1358(cals 323)	1309(cals 312)
GI RATING	Low	Low	Low	Low	Low	Low

Penang Chicken

SERVES: 4

500g skinless chicken breasts
1 medium sized onion
cooking spray
1 teaspoon crushed garlic (in jar)
1 teaspoon crushed ginger (in jar)
1 cup fresh green beans cut in half
2 cups zucchini sliced
2 cups small cauliflower florets
3 teaspoons Penang paste (in jar)
2 teaspoons fish sauce
1 tablespoon sugar
1 tablespoon fresh basil chopped
2 tablespoons cornflour
1 x 375ml can evaporated light milk
1 teaspoon imitation coconut essence
2½ tablespoons (20g) chopped unsalted peanuts (optional)

DIRECTIONS

Cut chicken into thin strips. Cut onion in quarters then slice thinly. Generously coat a large non-stick wok or frypan with cooking spray, sauté garlic and ginger and chicken until chicken is nearly cooked. Remove from pan and leave to one side. Coat wok or frypan again with cooking spray, sauté onion, beans, zucchini and cauliflower, cook 2 minutes. Add Penang paste, stir well, cook 3 to 5 minutes until vegetables are just cooked. Add fish sauce, sugar and basil. In a small mixing bowl combine cornflour, evaporated milk and coconut essence. Pour into pan, stir continuously until boiling. Serve with Basmati rice or noodles. Sprinkle chopped peanuts over top of each serve if desired.

VARIATION: OMIT PEANUTS AND REDUCE FAT COUNT BY 2.3g PER SERVE OR REPLACE CHICKEN WITH EITHER LEAN RUMP STEAK, BUTTERFLY PORK STEAKS, LEAN LAMB LEG STEAKS OR 400g TOFU DICED.

Dietitian's Tip
Coconut essence and evaporated milk provide a low saturated fat alternative to coconut milk.

Nutritional Information

PER SERVE	CHICKEN	RUMP	LAMB	PORK	TOFU
FAT TOTAL	7.5g	7.8g	7.3g	5.8g	10.6g
SATURATED	2.5g	3.1g	2.0g	2.1g	1.7g
FIBRE	2.8g	2.8g	2.8g	2.8g	2.6g
PROTEIN	40.3g	41.3g	40.6g	42.6g	22.0g
CARBS	21.8g	21.8g	21.8g	21.8g	25.7g
SUGAR	16.7g	16.7g	16.7g	16.7g	17.7g
SODIUM	417mg	410mg	412mg	428mg	354mg
KILOJOULES	1329(cals 316)	1360(cals 324)	1329(cals 316)	1308(cals 311)	1098(cals 261)
GI RATING	Low	Low	Low	Low	Low

Mooloolaba Chicken

SERVES: 4

250g peeled raw prawns
cooking spray
¼ teaspoon crushed garlic (in jar)
1 shallot chopped
2 tablespoons plain flour
½ cup skim milk
1 teaspoon fish sauce
4 x 125g skinless chicken breasts
4 toothpicks
1 egg white
3 tablespoons skim milk
¾ cup breadcrumbs (packet)

DIRECTIONS

Preheat oven 180°C fan forced. Chop prawns into small pieces. Coat a non-stick frypan with cooking spray, sauté prawns, garlic and shallots for 2 minutes. Blend flour with ½ cup skim milk, add to pan with fish sauce. Stir until thickened and mixture has boiled. Remove from heat and leave to cool. Using a sharp knife, make a pocket lengthways inside each chicken breast (don't cut all the way through). Use your finger to widen and open the hole to allow for filling. Once prawn mix has cooled spoon a quarter of the mixture into each chicken breast pocket. Push filling deep into breast. Seal opening with a toothpick. In a medium sized mixing bowl beat egg white with skim milk. Place breadcrumbs on a large dinner plate. Dip each chicken breast into egg mix, then coat chicken with breadcrumbs. Coat a baking tray with cooking spray, place chicken breasts on tray then spray chicken generously with cooking spray. Bake 25-30 minutes or until chicken is cooked through. Serve with potato or rice and with either salad or vegetables.

Dietitian's Tip
This is high in lean protein required for growth and repair of our cells throughout our life.

Nutritional Information

PER SERVE		
FAT	TOTAL	7.9g
	SATURATED	2.4g
FIBRE		0.8g
PROTEIN		44.5g
CARBS		13.5g
SUGAR		3.1g
SODIUM		555mg
KILOJOULES		1275(cals 304)
GI RATING		Medium

Homestead Chicken Pie

SERVES: 6

PIE FILLING

600g skinless chicken breasts

cooking spray

1 medium sized onion diced

250g mushrooms quartered

1½ cups skim milk

2 sachets cream of mushroom cup-a-soup (Continental®)

2 sachets cream of chicken cup-a-soup (Continental®)

2 tablespoons parsley chopped

pepper to taste

PIE TOP

1 tablespoon (15g) Flora Light® margarine

¼ cup skim milk

1 egg white

1 cup self raising flour

pinch of salt

Dietitian's Tip
Unlike many pies this is low in saturated fat and contains lean meat. I would recommend this for people with diabetes.

DIRECTIONS

Preheat oven 220°C fan forced.

To make pie filling: Cut chicken into bite sized pieces. Coat a large non-stick frypan with cooking spray, sauté chicken for 3 minutes. Add onion and cook 2 minutes. Add mushrooms and cook 2 minutes. Combine milk with soup mixes then pour into pan. Stir in parsley. Pepper to taste. Once mixture has boiled pour into a casserole dish. Leave to one side.

To make pie top: Melt margarine in microwave, add to milk and combine. Add egg white, beat with a fork until blended. In a medium sized mixing bowl put flour and salt, pour milk mixture into flour and combine. Turn onto a floured surface and roll out dough to the size of the casserole dish. Using a rolling pin, roll up pie top and lift onto top of filling. Trim edges and make a decorative edge by using the back of a fork, or pinch the edges with the tips of your fingers. Using a pastry brush, brush a little milk over top. Bake 10 minutes or until top is golden and cooked in the centre.

VARIATIONS: REPLACE CHICKEN WITH EITHER LEAN RUMP STEAK, LEAN LAMB LEG STEAKS, LEAN VEAL LEG STEAKS, BUTTERFLY PORK STEAKS OR 500g TOFU.

Nutritional Information

PER SERVE		CHICKEN	RUMP	LAMB	VEAL	PORK	TOFU
FAT	TOTAL	4.2g	4.5g	4.1g	2.2g	2.9g	6.9g
	SATURATED	1.0g	1.5g	1.4g	0.5g	0.7g	0.4g
FIBRE		2.3g	2.3g	2.3g	2.3g	2.3g	2.3g
PROTEIN		30.1g	30.9g	30.3g	28.6g	31.9g	15.8g
CARBS		22.4g	22.4g	22.4g	22.4g	22.4g	25.8g
SUGAR		4.8g	4.8g	4.8g	4.8g	4.8g	5.7g
SODIUM		348mg	343mg	357mg	374mg	345mg	298mg
KILOJOULES		1043(cals 248)	1068(cals 254)	1043(cals 248)	944(cals 225)	1026(cals 244)	870(cals 207)
GI RATING		Medium	Medium	Medium	Medium	Medium	Medium

Thai Chicken Stir-Fry

SERVES: 4

500g skinless chicken breasts
cooking spray
1 teaspoon crushed garlic (in jar)
1 teaspoon crushed ginger (in jar)
1 cup water
1½ cups carrots sliced
1½ cups small broccoli florets
1 cup onion diced
1 cup sugar snaps or snow peas
2 cups silverbeet/spinach sliced
⅓ cup Thai chilli jam (in jar)
2 teaspoons lemon grass (in jar)
1 tablespoon soy sauce 43% less salt
2 teaspoons salt reduced chicken-style stock powder (Massel®)
2 tablespoons cornflour

DIRECTIONS

Cut chicken into bite sized pieces. Coat a non-stick frypan or wok with cooking spray, sauté garlic, ginger and chicken for 3 minutes. Add ½ cup of water, carrots, broccoli and onion, cook 3 minutes. Add sugar snaps and spinach to pan, cook 3 minutes or until vegetables are cooked to your liking. Add chilli jam, lemon grass, soy sauce and chicken stock powder. Combine cornflour with remaining water, add to pan, stir continuously until sauce has boiled.

VARIATIONS: REPLACE CHICKEN WITH EITHER LEAN RUMP STEAK, BUTTERFLY PORK STEAK, LEAN LEG LAMB STEAKS OR 400g TOFU. ALL VARIATIONS SHOULD BE DICED.

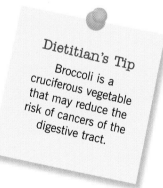

Dietitian's Tip
Broccoli is a cruciferous vegetable that may reduce the risk of cancers of the digestive tract.

Nutritional Information

PER SERVE		CHICKEN	RUMP	PORK	LAMB	TOFU
FAT	TOTAL	5.1g	5.5g	3.5g	5.0g	8.2g
	SATURATED	1.1g	1.7g	0.7g	1.6g	0.4g
FIBRE		4.2g	4.2g	4.2g	4.2g	4.2g
PROTEIN		32.6g	33.6g	34.9g	32.9g	14.4g
CARBS		14.5g	14.5g	14.5g	14.5g	18.6g
SUGAR		9.6g	9.6g	9.6g	9.6g	10.6g
SODIUM		546mg	540mg	542mg	557mg	483mg
KILOJOULES		990(cals 236)	1021(cals 243)	969(cals 231)	990(cals 236)	759 (cals 181)
GI RATING		Medium	Medium	Medium	Medium	Medium

Rippa Rissoles

SERVES: 6

½ cup raw brown rice

¾ cup carrots grated

¾ cup zucchini grated

1 small onion finely diced

500g very lean beef mince

1 teaspoon beef stock powder

2 tablespoons oyster sauce

1 sachet spring vegetable cup-a-soup (Continental®)

1 egg white

pepper to taste

cooking spray

DIRECTIONS

Follow cooking instructions on rice packet. Rinse and drain well. Place vegetables in a large mixing bowl. Add all remaining ingredients including cooked rice to bowl and combine well. Use your hands to achieve a good consistency with rissoles. Shape into 12 patties. If time permits refrigerate rissoles for a few hours before cooking. Generously coat a large non-stick frypan with cooking spray, fry rissoles 3 to 5 minutes on each side or until cooked through and browned on both sides.

VARIATIONS: REPLACE BEEF MINCE WITH EITHER LEAN CHICKEN MINCE, LEAN LAMB MINCE OR LEAN PORK MINCE.

Dietitian's Tip

Adding rice and vegetables to rissoles will lower the total fat and provide dietary fibre required for normal bowel function.

Sticky Pork Chops

SERVES: 4

⅓ cup plum sauce (in jar)

2 teaspoons sweet chilli sauce

1 tablespoon soy sauce 43% less salt

2 tablespoons honey

cooking spray

4 x 175g lean mid loin pork chops

½ teaspoon crushed garlic (in jar)

½ teaspoon crushed ginger (in jar)

⅛ teaspoon Chinese 5 spice

DIRECTIONS

In a small bowl combine plum, sweet chilli and soy sauces, and honey. Coat a large non-stick frypan with cooking spray, fry pork chops until cooked to your liking. Remove chops onto a large dinner plate, leave to one side. Re-spray frypan with cooking spray and sauté garlic, ginger, honey mixture and Chinese 5 spice, mixing well. Once boiled, simmer for 2 minutes. Return chops to pan to reheat and coat with sauce.

VARIATIONS: REPLACE PORK WITH EITHER 4 x 150g SKINLESS CHICKEN BREASTS, 4 x 150g LEAN RUMP STEAKS OR 400g TOFU CUT INTO 4 SLICES

Dietitian's Tip

The honey adds flavour and small quantities can be include in the eating plan for people with diabetes.

Nutritional Information

PER SERVE		BEEF	CHICKEN	LAMB	PORK
FAT	TOTAL	6.4g	7.4g	6.4g	6.5g
	SATURATED	2.6g	2.1g	2.7g	2.3g
FIBRE		1.6g	1.6g	1.6g	1.6g
PROTEIN		19.7g	18.8g	19.8g	19.4g
CARBS		16.9g	16.9g	16.9g	16.9g
SUGAR		3.0g	3.0g	3.0g	3.0g
SODIUM		434mg	446mg	441mg	435mg
KILOJOULES		857(cals 204)	879(cals 209)	859(cals 204)	856(cals 204)
GI RATING		High	High	High	High

Nutritional Information

PER SERVE		PORK	CHICKEN	RUMP	TOFU
FAT	TOTAL	3.0g	3.5g	3.9g	6.0g
	SATURATED	1.1g	0.9g	1.7g	0g
FIBRE		0.1g	0.1g	0.1g	0.1g
PROTEIN		40.8g	34.3g	35.5g	10.4g
CARBS		10.4g	10.4g	10.4g	14.4g
SUGAR		8.9g	8.9g	8.9g	9.9g
SODIUM		422m	378mg	371mg	302mg
KILOJOULES		1140(cals 271)	1046(cals 249)	1083(cals 258)	697(cals 166)
GI RATING		Low	Low	Low	Low

Symple Beef Sticks

MAKES: 12 STICKS

500g very lean beef mince

⅓ cup onion grated

½ teaspoon crushed garlic (in jar)

2 tablespoons tomato sauce

2 tablespoons barbecue sauce

1 teaspoon beef stock powder

1 egg white

pepper to taste

¼ cup breadcrumbs (packet)

12 wooden kebab sticks

cooking spray

Dietitian's Tip
The Australian Dietary Guidelines recommend that lean red meat be eaten three times a week providing iron for oxygen transport throughout the body.

DIRECTIONS

Soak Kebab sticks in water before use to avoid burning. In a large mixing bowl combine all ingredients except the breadcrumbs, kebab sticks and cooking spray. Use your hands to work the mixture together until well combined. Divide mixture into 12 (mince for each kebab should weigh around 58 grams). Roll each piece out into a long sausage shape, coat generously in breadcrumbs. Push the kebab stick through the centre of meat, not going all the way to the end (leave about 6cms of stick so you can hold kebab in your hand). Refrigerate for a few hours if possible. Cook kebabs on the flat top part of the barbecue or under griller. Spray flat top of barbecue with cooking spray. BE CAREFUL NOT TO GET SPRAY NEAR AN OPEN FLAME! Turn sticks to cook evenly, spraying lightly with cooking spray each turn.

VARIATIONS: REPLACE BEEF MINCE WITH EITHER LEAN CHICKEN MINCE, LEAN LAMB MINCE, LEAN PORK MINCE.

Nutritional Information

PER STICK		BEEF	CHICKEN	LAMB	PORK
FAT	TOTAL	3.0g	3.5g	3.0g	3.0g
	SATURATED	1.2g	1.0g	1.3g	1.1g
FIBRE		0.3g	0.3g	0.3g	0.3g
PROTEIN		9.2g	8.7g	9.2g	9.1g
CARBS		3.4g	3.4g	3.4g	3.4g
SUGAR		2.1g	2.1g	2.1g	2.1g
SODIUM		149mg	155mg	152mg	149mg
KILOJOULES		324(cals 77)	334(cals 79)	324(cals 77)	323(cals 77)
GI RATING		*Not available due to the low carb content*			

Tasty Meat Loaf

SERVES: 6

⅓ cup raw brown rice

3 slices multigrain bread

⅓ cup skim milk

½ cup carrots grated

½ cup zucchini grated

½ cup capsicum finely diced

2 tablespoons oyster sauce

1 small onion finely diced

500g very lean beef mince

2 egg whites

½ teaspoon dried mixed herbs

1 sachet Garden Harvest creamy mushroom cup-a-soup (Continental®)

2 teaspoons salt reduced chicken-style stock powder (Massel®)

pepper to taste

cooking spray

Dietitian's Tip
Adding rice, bread & vegetables to a meat loaf provides fibre & decreases the amount of meat in the recipe. This will decrease the total kilojoule intake making it suitable for overweight people with diabetes.

DIRECTIONS

Preheat oven 180°C fan forced. Follow cooking instructions on rice packet, rinse and drain well, leave to one side. In a small bowl soak bread with milk, leave to one side. Place vegetables into a large mixing bowl then add all remaining ingredients into bowl including cooked rice and bread, mix well. Use your hands to achieve a good consistency with mixture. Coat a large loaf tin with cooking spray, press mixture into tin, flatten top. Bake 60 minutes.

VARIATIONS: REPLACE BEEF WITH EITHER LEAN CHICKEN MINCE, LEAN LAMB MINCE OR LEAN PORK MINCE.

Nutritional Information

PER SERVE		BEEF	CHICKEN	LAMB	PORK
FAT	TOTAL	6.6g	7.6g	6.6g	6.7g
	SATURATED	2.6g	2.2g	2.8g	2.3g
FIBRE		2.0g	2.0g	2.0g	2.0g
PROTEIN		21.7g	20.8g	21.8g	21.4g
CARBS		19.4g	19.4g	19.4g	19.4g
SUGAR		4.5g	4.5g	4.5g	4.5g
SODIUM		407mg	419mg	414mg	408mg
KILOJOULES		943(cals 224)	964(cals 229)	944(cals 225)	942(cals 224)
GI RATING		Medium	Medium	Medium	Medium

Marinated BBQ Steak

SERVES: 6

6 x 150g lean raw rump steaks
MARINADE
½ cup dry white wine
2 tablespoons no added salt tomato paste
¼ cup Thai chilli jam paste (in jar)
1 teaspoon crushed garlic (in jar)
1 teaspoon crushed ginger (in jar)

DIRECTIONS

Trim fat from rump. In a medium sized bowl combine all marinade ingredients. Place steaks into a flat container that has a lid, pour marinade over steaks. Place lid on top and refrigerate. Turn steaks occasionally. Marinate steaks overnight if possible, or for at least 4 hours. When ready to cook, remove steak from marinade and either barbecue or grill to your liking. Pour remaining marinade over steaks while cooking.

ANNETTE'S TIP: When barbecuing steak, only turn meat once to avoid drying out.

VARIATION: REPLACE RUMP WITH EITHER SKINLESS CHICKEN BREASTS, BUTTERFLY PORK STEAKS, OR 600g TOFU

Dietitian's Tip
Barbecuing the steak with this marinade produces a lean, low salt steak suitable for those with heart concerns.

Pork with Apple Glaze

SERVES: 4

4 x 175g lean mid loin pork chops
2 green apples
cooking spray
⅓ cup brown sugar loosely packed
¼ cup brandy
½ cup apple sauce (in jar)
1 teaspoon cornflour
1 tablespoon water

Dietitian's Tip
A great way to include fruit into your eating plan. The Australian Dietary Guidelines recommend 2 serves of fruit a day.

DIRECTIONS

Cut as much visible fat from pork chops as possible. Peel and core apples, cut in half then cut into slices. Coat a large non-stick frypan with cooking spray, add sugar and apple. Allow apple to brown with sugar, cook both sides. Once apple is cooked remove from pan onto a small plate, leave to one side. Coat frypan with cooking spray (don't wash it as you want the flavours of the sugar and apple to stay in the pan), once pan is hot, fry chops. Move chops around to absorb any left over sugar. Cook each side for about 3 to 5 minutes depending on how well done you like the chops. Turn once during cooking (turning frequently dries out meat). Once cooked remove onto a large dinner plate. Pour brandy into frypan and cook for 30 seconds, add apple sauce. Combine cornflour with water and pour into pan, stir continuously to avoid lumps. Once boiled, reduce and simmer 2 minutes. Return chops to pan and reheat covering with sauce. To serve, pour ¼ of sauce over chop and place ¼ of the apple slices on top.

Nutritional Information

PER SERVE	RUMP	CHICKEN	PORK	TOFU
FAT TOTAL	5.0g	4.5g	2.6g	7.1g
SATURATED	1.8g	1.1g	0.6g	0.2g
FIBRE	0.1g	0.1g	0.1g	0.1g
PROTEIN	35.8g	34.6g	37.3g	10.7g
CARBS	3.9g	3.9g	3.9g	7.9g
SUGAR	3.5g	3.5g	3.5g	4.5g
SODIUM	230mg	237mg	233mg	161mg
KILOJOULES	918(cals 319)	880(cals 209)	855(cals 204)	532(cals 127)
GI RATING	*Not available due to the low carb content*			

Nutritional Information

PER SERVE	
FAT TOTAL	3.2g
SATURATED	1.1g
FIBRE	1.4g
PROTEIN	40.8g
CARBS	20.7g
SUGAR	19.5g
SODIUM	314mg
KILOJOULES	1277(cals 304)
GI RATING	Medium

Moussaka

SERVES: 6

2 medium sized eggplants (1 kilo)

cooking spray

MEAT SAUCE

500g very lean lamb mince

1 cup onion diced

1 teaspoon crushed garlic (in jar)

2 teaspoons beef stock powder

2 tablespoons no added salt tomato paste

1 x 410g can tomato puree

1 x 425g can crushed tomatoes

2 tablespoons fresh mint chopped

WHITE SAUCE

1 tablespoon (15g) Flora Light® margarine

3 tablespoons plain flour

2 cups skim milk

1 x 30g sachet 4 cheese sauce (Continental®)

TOPPING

½ cup 25% reduced fat grated tasty cheese

DIRECTIONS

Preheat oven 200ºC fan forced.

Cut unpeeled eggplant lengthways into 1cm slices. Generously coat a large non-stick frypan with cooking spray, fry sliced eggplant for 1 to 2 minutes on each side until slightly browned. Spray pan each time you add more eggplant slices. Leave to one side.

To make meat sauce: Coat the same frypan with cooking spray, sauté mince until cooked, drain off any liquid. Add onion and garlic to pan and cook 3 minutes. Add all remaining ingredients. Once boiled simmer 5 minutes. Leave to one side.

To make white sauce: In a medium sized saucepan melt margarine, add flour and stir together well. Slowly add milk, using a whisk to avoid lumps. Stir continuously. Once boiled add cheese sauce sachet using a whisk to keep smooth. Leave to one side.

To assemble moussaka: You will need 3 layers of eggplant slices so divide cooked eggplant into 3 portions. Coat a lasagne dish with cooking spray, place a layer of eggplant on base. Cover with ½ meat sauce then another layer of eggplant slices. Top with remaining meat sauce then cover with remaining eggplant slices. Spread white sauce over top then sprinkle grated cheese over sauce. Bake 30-35 minutes.

VARIATION: REPLACE LAMB MINCE WITH LEAN BEEF

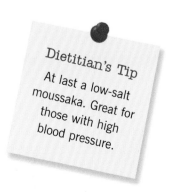

Dietitian's Tip

At last a low-salt moussaka. Great for those with high blood pressure.

Nutritional Information

PER SERVE		LAMB	BEEF
FAT	TOTAL	7.6g	7.6g
	SATURATED	3.2g	3.1g
FIBRE		4.8g	4.8g
PROTEIN		20.0g	19.9g
CARBS		13.8g	13.8g
SUGAR		10.9g	10.9g
SODIUM		427mg	421mg
KILOJOULES		854(cals 203)	853(cals 203)
GI RATING		Low	Low

Eastern Lamb

SERVES: 4

2 cups raw pumpkin

500g raw lean lamb leg steaks

1 cup red capsicum cut into strips

1 cup fresh green beans cut in half

½ cup shallots cut into 2cm pieces

cooking spray

3 teaspoons red curry paste (in jar)

1 teaspoon crushed garlic (in jar)

1 teaspoon crushed ginger (in jar)

2 teaspoons salt reduced chicken-style stock powder (Massel®)

2 teaspoons soy sauce

1 tablespoon fresh coriander chopped

2 teaspoons sugar

2 tablespoons cornflour

1 x 375ml can evaporated light milk

½ teaspoon imitation coconut essence

DIRECTIONS

Peel pumpkin then dice into medium sized pieces. Microwave in a little water until just cooked but still firm (don't overcook pumpkin as it will go mushy). Drain, leave to one side. Cut lamb into thin strips. Coat a large non-stick wok or frypan with cooking spray, sauté lamb with red curry paste, garlic and ginger until lamb is almost cooked. Add vegetables, toss with meat until vegetables are cooked to your liking. Place stock powder, soy sauce, coriander and sugar into pan and stir well. Combine cornflour with milk and essence then pour into pan, stir continuously until boiled. Gently fold pumpkin through dish, cook until pumpkin is heated through.

VARIATIONS: REPLACE LAMB WITH EITHER SKINLESS CHICKEN BREASTS, LEAN RUMP STEAKS, LEAN BUTTERFLY PORK STEAKS OR 400g TOFU.

Dietitian's Tip

This low fat recipe combines pumpkin high in vitamin A and fibre and meat high in protein, iron and zinc. Excellent for people with diabetes.

Nutritional Information

PER SERVE	LAMB	CHICKEN	STEAK	PORK	TOFU
FAT TOTAL	5.2g	5.3g	5.7g	3.7g	8.4g
SATURATED	2.6g	2.1g	2.7g	1.7g	1.3g
FIBRE	2.4g	2.4g	2.4g	2.4g	2.4g
PROTEIN	39.7g	39.4g	40.4g	41.7g	21.2g
CARBS	23.6g	23.6g	23.6g	23.6g	27.6g
SUGAR	17.9g	17.9g	17.9g	17.9g	18.9g
SODIUM	407mg	396mg	390mg	392mg	333mg
KILOJOULES	1264(cals 301)	1264(cals 301)	1295(cals 308)	1243(cals 296)	1033(cals 246)
GI RATING	Low	Low	Low	Low	Low

Moroccan Savoury Mince

SERVES: 4

cooking spray

500g lean lamb mince

1 teaspoon crushed garlic (in jar)

2 teaspoons Moroccan seasoning

1 teaspoon cinnamon

1 x 415g can no added salt chopped tomatoes

2 teaspoons salt reduced chicken-style stock powder (Massel®)

1 tablespoon no added salt tomato paste

¼ cup lemon juice

1 teaspoon grated fresh lemon rind

1 x 400g can chickpeas drained

1 cup peeled apple diced

3 tablespoons fresh mint chopped

½ cup water

⅛ teaspoon chilli powder (optional)

Dietitian's Tip
Buy the Heart Foundation ticked mince. This is less than 10% fat and suitable to include in meals for people with diabetes.

DIRECTIONS

Coat a large non-stick saucepan with cooking spray, sauté mince until cooked. Drain liquid from mince. Add garlic, Moroccan seasoning and cinnamon, combine. Add all remaining ingredients to pot, stir well. Once boiled simmer for 10 minutes. Serve with couscous, rice or potato.

VARIATIONS: REPLACE LAMB MINCE WITH EITHER LEAN BEEF MINCE, LEAN CHICKEN MINCE OR LEAN PORK MINCE.

Nutritional Information

PER SERVE		LAMB	BEEF	CHICKEN	PORK
FAT	TOTAL	10.1g	10.1g	11.6g	10.3g
	SATURATED	4.1g	3.8g	3.2g	3.4g
FIBRE		4.4g	4.4g	4.4g	4.4g
PROTEIN		30.6g	30.5g	29.1g	30.1g
CARBS		16.4g	16.4g	16.4g	16.4g
SUGAR		7.0g	7.0g	7.0g	7.0g
SODIUM		334mg	323mg	342mg	326mg
KILOJOULES		1170(cals 278)	1168(cals 278)	1200(cals 286)	1166(cals 278)
GI RATING		Low	Low	Low	Low

Steak with Creamy Mustard Sauce

SERVES: 6

6 x 150g lean rump steaks

cooking spray

1 tablespoon cornflour

1 x 375ml can evaporated light milk

¼ cup shallots chopped

¼ cup wholegrain mustard (Masterfoods®)

1 teaspoon French mustard (in jar)

¼ cup brandy

½ teaspoon Worcestershire sauce

1 teaspoon salt reduced chicken-style stock powder (Massel®)

pepper to taste

DIRECTIONS

Cut as much fat from steak as possible. Coat a large non-stick frypan with cooking spray, fry steaks to your liking. Remove and put on a plate, leave to one side. In a small mixing bowl combine cornflour with evaporated milk, leave to one side. Re-use frypan (don't wash it as you want the flavours of the meat to stay in the pan). Add shallots and both mustards, sauté 30 seconds stir well. Add brandy, Worcestershire sauce and stock powder. Cook for 1 minute. Add milk mixture, combine well. Pepper to taste. Return steaks to pan and reheat in sauce.

VARIATIONS: REPLACE RUMP WITH EITHER LEAN BUTTERFLY PORK STEAKS, LEAN LAMB LEG STEAKS OR SKINLESS CHICKEN BREASTS.

Nutritional Information

PER SERVE		RUMP	PORK	LAMB	CHICKEN
FAT	TOTAL	5.9g	3.5g	5.3g	5.5g
	SATURATED	2.4g	1.2g	2.2g	1.6g
FIBRE		0.1g	0.1g	0.1g	0.1g
PROTEIN		41.3g	42.8g	40.4g	40.1g
CARBS		10.5g	10.5g	10.5g	10.5g
SUGAR		7.9g	7.9g	7.9g	7.9g
SODIUM		401mg	404mg	422mg	408mg
KILOJOULES		1183(cals 282)	1120(cals 267)	1145(cals 273)	1145(cals 273)
GI RATING		Low	Low	Low	Low

Oriental Pork

SERVES: 4

500g butterfly pork steaks

cooking spray

2 teaspoons crushed ginger (in jar)

1 cup celery sliced

1 cup fresh green beans sliced

1 cup onion sliced

¾ cup fresh baby corn cut in half

1 cup capsicum sliced

2 teaspoons salt reduced chicken-style stock powder (Massel®)

1 tablespoon soy sauce 43% less salt

1 teaspoon fish sauce

2 teaspoons sweet chilli sauce

2 tablespoons crunchy peanut butter

1 tablespoon cornflour

1 x 375ml can evaporated light milk

½ teaspoon imitation coconut essence

DIRECTIONS

Cut pork into thin strips. Coat a large non-stick frypan or wok with cooking spray, sauté pork and ginger until browned. Add celery, beans, onion, corn and capsicum and cook 4 to 5 minutes or until vegetables are cooked to your liking. Add stock powder, soy, fish and sweet chilli sauces, and peanut butter and blend well. In a small mixing bowl combine cornflour with evaporated milk and coconut essence then pour into pan, stir continuously until boiling.

VARIATIONS: REPLACE PORK WITH EITHER RUMP STEAK, SKINLESS CHICKEN BREASTS OR LEAN LEG LAMB STEAKS OR 400g TOFU, OR TO REDUCE THE SODIUM COUNT REPLACE CRUNCHY PEANUT BUTTER WITH NO ADDED SALT CRUNCHY PEANUT BUTTER.

Dietitian's Tip

Butterfly pork is low in fat and high in B vitamins required for normal cell function.

Nutritional Information

PER SERVE		PORK	RUMP	CHICKEN	LAMB	TOFU
FAT	TOTAL	8.0g	10.0g	9.6g	9.5g	12.7g
	SATURATED	2.2g	3.2g	2.6g	3.1g	1.9g
FIBRE		3.8g	3.8g	3.8g	3.8g	3.8g
PROTEIN		43.9g	42.7g	41.7g	41.9g	23.4g
CARBS		24.7g	24.7g	24.7g	24.7g	28.7g
SUGAR		15.5g	15.5g	15.5g	15.5g	16.5g
SODIUM		570mg	568mg	574mg	585mg	511mg
KILOJOULES		1459(cals 347)	1512(cals 360)	1481(cals 353)	1481(cals 353)	1249(cals 297)
GI RATING	*Not available due to the low carb content*					

Party Food

Serve all dips with either sliced vegetables eg. celery, carrot, cucumber, Corn Chips (Book 1) or Rice Crackers, low fat Jatz or Cruskits cut into large squares.

Clockwise from top centre: French Onion, Roasted Capsicum, Creamy Smoked Salmon, Hommus, Tijuana Bean, Corn Relish, Cheese & Chive and Savoury Tuna Dip.

Cheese and Chive Dip

SERVES: 20

250g low fat cottage cheese
½ cup 25% reduced fat grated tasty cheese
2 tablespoons fresh chives chopped

DIRECTIONS

In a food processor beat cottage cheese until very smooth. Add cheese and beat until well combined. Add chives and beat for a few seconds until blended into mixture. Keep refrigerated. Best made a few hours ahead.

Nutritional Information

PER SERVE (approx 1 tablespoon)

FAT TOTAL	0.8g		SUGAR	0.3g
SATURATED	0.5g		SODIUM	34mg
FIBRE	0g		KILOJOULES	82(cals 19)
PROTEIN	2.9g		GI RATING	*Not available due to*
CARBS	0.3g			*the low carb content*

French Onion Dip

SERVES: 20

250g low fat cottage cheese
1 teaspoon lemon juice
1 tablespoon dried French onion soup (Continental®)

DIRECTIONS

In a food processor beat cottage cheese until very smooth. Add in lemon juice and dried soup mix. Beat until well combined. Keep refrigerated. Best made a few hours ahead.

Nutritional Information

PER SERVE (approx 1 tablespoon)

FAT TOTAL	0.2g		SUGAR	0.2g
SATURATED	0.1g		SODIUM	19mg
FIBRE	0g		KILOJOULES	47(cals 11)
PROTEIN	2.2g		GI RATING	*Not available due to*
CARBS	0.3g			*the low carb content*

Hommus

SERVES: 20

1 x 400g can chickpeas drained
1 tablespoon lemon juice
1 tablespoon 97% fat-free mayonnaise (Kraft®)
½ teaspoon crushed garlic (in jar)
¼ cup water
½ teaspoon salt reduced vegetable stock powder (Massel®)
pepper to taste

DIRECTIONS

In a food processor beat chickpeas for 1 to 2 minutes until mashed. Add all other ingredients and process until mixture becomes a smooth paste. Keep refrigerated. Best made a few hours ahead.

Nutritional Information

PER SERVE (approx 1 tablespoon)

FAT TOTAL	0.3g		SUGAR	0.3g
SATURATED	0g		SODIUM	35mg
FIBRE	0.6g		KILOJOULES	53(cals 13)
PROTEIN	0.7g		GI RATING	Low
CARBS	1.8g			

Creamy Smoked Salmon Dip

SERVES: 20

75g smoked salmon (Royal Tasmanian®)
250g low fat cottage cheese
1 teaspoon lemon juice
1 gherkin finely diced (in jar)

DIRECTIONS

Cut salmon into strips. In a food processor beat cottage cheese until very smooth. Add salmon, lemon juice and gherkin and beat until well combined. Keep refrigerated. Best made a few hours ahead.

Nutritional Information

PER SERVE (approx 1 tablespoon)

FAT TOTAL	0.6g		SUGAR	0.4g
SATURATED	0.2g		SODIUM	52mg
FIBRE	0g		KILOJOULES	81(cals 19)
PROTEIN	2.3g		GI RATING	*Not available due to the*
CARBS	0.5g			*low carb content*

Tijuana Bean Dip

SERVES: 20

250g low fat cottage cheese
1 x 400g can 4 bean mix drained and rinsed
1 tablespoon reduced salt taco seasoning (Old El Paso®)
1 tablespoon no added salt tomato paste
pepper to taste

DIRECTIONS

In a food processor beat cottage cheese until very smooth. Add beans, taco seasoning and tomato paste, beat until well combined. Keep refrigerated. Best made a few hours ahead.

Nutritional Information

PER SERVE (approx 1 tablespoon)

FAT TOTAL	0.2g		SUGAR	0.7g
SATURATED	0.1g		SODIUM	72mg
FIBRE	0.8g		KILOJOULES	94(cals 22)
PROTEIN	3.0g		GI RATING	Low
CARBS	2.1g			

Savoury Tuna Dip

SERVES: 20

250g low fat cottage cheese
2 x 100g cans Tuna Tempters onion & tomato savoury sauce (John West®)

DIRECTIONS

In a food processor beat cottage cheese until very smooth. Add both cans of tuna and beat until blended into mixture. Keep refrigerated. Best made a few hours ahead.

Nutritional Information

PER SERVE (approx 1 tablespoon)

FAT TOTAL	0.6g		SUGAR	0.6g
SATURATED	0.2g		SODIUM	56mg
FIBRE	0g		KILOJOULES	106(cals 25)
PROTEIN	4.3g		GI RATING	*Not available due to the*
CARBS	0.7g			*low carb content*

Corn Relish Dip

SERVES: 20

250g low fat cottage cheese

¾ cup corn relish (Masterfoods®)

DIRECTIONS

In a food processor beat cottage cheese until very smooth. Add relish, beat until well combined. Keep refrigerated. Best made a few hours ahead.

Nutritional Information

PER SERVE (approx 1 tablespoon)			
FAT TOTAL	0.2g	SUGAR	1.9g
SATURATED	0.1g	SODIUM	52mg
FIBRE	0g	KILOJOULES	87(cals 21)
PROTEIN	2.3g	GI RATING	Medium
CARBS	2.5g		

Roasted Capsicum Dip

SERVES: 20

300g red capsicum

cooking spray

250g low fat cottage cheese

30g semi-sundried tomatoes diced

½ teaspoon chicken stock powder

1 tablespoon Spanish olives diced (optional)

DIRECTIONS

To roast capsicum, cut in large slices, removing core and seeds. Coat slices with cooking spray and place under griller. Grill both sides until browned. Skin side will blister. Allow to cool then peel outside skin from capsicum and throw skin away. In a food processor beat cottage cheese until very smooth. Add capsicum and blend into mixture. Add sundried tomatoes, stock powder and olives (optional), mix ingredients until blended. Keep refrigerated. Best made a few hours ahead.

Nutritional Information

PER SERVE (approx 1 tablespoon)			
FAT TOTAL	0.5g	SUGAR	0.5g
SATURATED	0.1g	SODIUM	37mg
FIBRE	0.1g	KILOJOULES	77(cals 18)
PROTEIN	2.5g	GI RATING	Not available due to the low carb content
CARBS	0.9g		

Cheese and Spinach Triangles

MAKES: 24 TRIANGLES

1 x 250g packet frozen chopped spinach

50g reduced fat feta cheese

1 cup 25% reduced fat grated tasty cheese

2 tablespoons grated parmesan cheese

¼ cup onion finely diced

½ teaspoon crushed garlic (in jar)

pinch of nutmeg

6 sheets filo pastry (Antoniou®)

cooking spray

Dietitian's Tip

Spinach is high in B vitamins and minerals and included in filo pastry is suitable as a snack for a person with diabetes.

DIRECTIONS

Preheat oven 200°C fan forced. **To make filling:** Defrost spinach and squeeze out as much liquid as possible. In a medium sized mixing bowl crumble feta, add spinach and all other ingredients except the filo pastry and cooking spray. Mix together well.

To make triangles: Using one filo sheet at a time cut into 4 long strips, spray pastry with cooking spray. Place a tablespoon of mixture onto top corner of one strip then fold mixture over to other side diagonally. Continue folding diagonally until you reach the end of the strip. Coat a large baking tray with cooking spray, place triangle on tray. Repeat this method until 24 triangles are made. Coat with cooking spray. Bake 15-20 minutes or until lightly browned. Serve immediately as the pastry will soften when cooled.

Nutritional Information

PER TRIANGLE	
FAT TOTAL	1.6g
SATURATED	1.0g
FIBRE	0.6g
PROTEIN	2.6g
CARBS	2.0g
SUGAR	0.2g
SODIUM	98mg
KILOJOULES	140(cals 33)
GI RATING	High

Savoury Bread Cases

MAKES: 24 CASES

BREAD CASES
24 slices white bread
cooking spray
FILLING
½ cup onion diced or shallots sliced
1 x 420g can corn kernels drained
1 x 420g can creamed corn
1 teaspoon reduced salt vegetable stock
powder (Massel®)

DIRECTIONS

Preheat oven 180°C fan forced.

To make bread cases: Make a round shape with bread slices using either a glass that measures 9cm at the rim or a 9cm scone cutter. Press firmly over bread and push cutter down, remove crusts. Coat a 12 hole muffin tin with cooking spray and push a slice of bread into each hole. Bake 20-25 minutes or until crisp. Remove from pan then repeat process with the other 12 slices of bread.

To make filling: Coat a medium sized saucepan with cooking spray, sauté onion for 2 minutes. Add remaining ingredients and bring to boil. Simmer 3 minutes. Spoon filling into each bread case and serve.

VARIATIONS: REPLACE CORN FILLING WITH OTHER RECIPES FROM MY COOKBOOKS.

ANNETTE'S TIP: For a lower GI Rating replace white bread with multigrain bread.

Nutritional Information

PER CASE	CORN/CASE	CASE ONLY
FAT TOTAL	0.7g	0.5g
SATURATED	0.1g	0.1g
FIBRE	1.5g	0.5g
PROTEIN	2.2g	1.5g
CARBS	13.1g	8.1g
SUGAR	1.8g	0.4g
SODIUM	213mg	92mg
KILOJOULES	286(cals 68)	180(cals 43)
GI RATING	Medium	Medium

Mini Meat Tucker Bags

MAKES: 40 BAGS

cooking spray
500g very lean beef mince
½ cup onion finely diced
3 tablespoons Gravox® Lite Supreme
2 teaspoons beef stock powder
2 tablespoons tomato sauce
¾ cup water
20 sheets filo pastry
(Antoniou®)

Dietitian's Tip
Using filo pastry with lean beef mince provides a low fat snack.

DIRECTIONS

To make filling: Coat a medium sized saucepan with cooking spray, fry mince until cooked and drain excess liquid. Sauté onion with mince, cook 2 minutes. Add all remaining ingredients except filo pastry, bring to boil, stir continuously. Leave to cool. Preheat oven 200°C fan forced. **To prepare tucker bags:** Lay out one sheet of filo pastry. Coat with cooking spray. Cut sheet in half widthways. Place one cut half on top of the other one. Now cut sheet in half again. Using one half for each tucker bag, put a tablespoon of mixture into centre of each square, lift edges up over filling. Using the tips of your fingers, squeeze pastry over top of filling to hold mixture in (squeeze tightly and it will make the shape shown in picture). Each spoonful of mixture weighs about 30 grams. Repeat this with remaining sheets of pastry and mixture to make a total of 40 tucker bags. Coat a baking tray with cooking spray, place bags on tray then coat with cooking spray. Bake 15-20 minutes or until golden brown. Serve immediately as pastry will soften slightly when left to cool.

VARIATION: REPLACE WITH LEAN CHICKEN MINCE.

Nutritional Information

PER BAG	BEEF	CHICKEN
FAT TOTAL	1.1g	1.2g
SATURATED	0.4g	0.3g
FIBRE	0.2g	0.2g
PROTEIN	3.3g	3.1g
CARBS	4.2g	4.2g
SUGAR	0.3g	0.3g
SODIUM	106mg	108mg
KILOJOULES	165(cals 39)	168(cals 40)
GI RATING	*Not available due to the low carb content*	

Ming Rolls

MAKES: 36 ROLLS

cooking spray
500g very lean beef mince
1 medium sized onion diced
1 teaspoon crushed garlic (in jar)
1 teaspoon dried coriander
1 teaspoon turmeric
1 teaspoon cumin
¼ teaspoon dried chilli powder
1 x 40g packet chicken noodle soup (Continental®)
½ cup raw Basmati rice
3 cups water
4 cups cabbage finely shredded
18 sheets filo pastry (Antoniou®)

DIRECTIONS

To make filling: Coat a large non-stick frypan (that has a lid) with cooking spray, fry mince until nearly cooked. Drain liquid. Add onion and garlic, cook 2 minutes. Add coriander, turmeric, cumin, chilli powder, soup mix, raw rice and water, stir well. Top with cabbage. Lower temperature slightly so that mixture doesn't burn, place lid on top and allow cabbage to steam for 5 minutes. Fold cabbage through meat, put lid back on and cook 4 to 5 minutes or until rice has cooked through. Leave to cool.

Preheat oven 200ºC fan forced.

To make rolls: Lay out one sheet of filo pastry widthways and coat with cooking spray. Cut down the centre of sheet, which will give you 2 halves. Place one sheet on top of the other, cut in half down centre like before giving you 2 sheets. In the middle of the edge closest to you place 2 dessertspoons of mixture on each sheet. Spray with cooking spray then fold right and left edges in. Roll away from yourself, rolling tightly and keeping edges folded in to avoid mixture falling out. Repeat with other sheet. The shape should be similar to a spring roll. Repeat this method until 36 rolls are made (2 rolls per sheet of filo pastry). Coat a baking tray with cooking spray, place rolls on tray then coat with cooking spray. Bake 25-30 minutes or until lightly browned. Serve immediately as the pastry will soften when cooled. Serve with dipping sauces, or sweet chilli, soy or tomato sauces.

VARIATIONS:
REPLACE BEEF MINCE WITH LEAN CHICKEN MINCE OR LEAN PORK MINCE.

Dietitian's Tip
A great low fat choice instead of deep fried spring rolls.

Nutritional Information

PER ROLL		BEEF	CHICKEN	PORK
FAT	TOTAL	1.2g	1.3g	1.2g
	SATURATED	0.4g	0.4g	0.4g
FIBRE		0.6g	0.6g	0.6g
PROTEIN		3.9g	3.7g	3.9g
CARBS		6.6g	6.6g	6.6g
SUGAR		0.5g	0.5g	0.5g
SODIUM		65mg	68mg	66mg
KILOJOULES		220(cals 52)	224(cals 53)	220(cals 52)
GI RATING		High	High	High

Mini Quiches

MAKES: 24

PASTRY

1¼ cups plain flour

½ cup self raising flour

⅓ cup skim milk

1 egg white

2 tablespoons Flora Light® margarine melted

FILLING

cooking spray

¾ cup (110g) bacon short cuts diced

2 whole eggs plus 2 egg whites

1 cup skim milk

3 tablespoons grated parmesan cheese

¼ cup fresh parsley finely chopped

½ teaspoon crushed garlic (in jar)

½ cup 25% reduced fat grated tasty cheese

DIRECTIONS

Preheat oven 180°C fan forced. **To make pastry:** In a large mixing bowl sift both flours. Combine milk and egg white, beat with a fork. Add melted margarine, then add milk mixture to flour and fold together. Leave to one side.

To make filling: Coat a small non-stick frypan with cooking spray, fry bacon until browned. Leave to one side. In a medium sized mixing bowl beat eggs and whites for 1 minute using an electric beater. Add milk and beat until blended. Add parmesan cheese, parsley, garlic, grated cheese and cooked bacon.

To prepare quiches: On a well-floured surface roll out pastry until fairly thin. Using an 8cm scone cutter cut 24 circles. Coat a 12 holed muffin tin with cooking spray and place 12 pastry bases into holes. Pour egg mixture to reach nearly the top of pastry. Bake 20-25 minutes or until egg mixture is firm in centre. Repeat with other 12 pastry bases and filling. Serve hot or cold.

VARIATION: FOR A VEGETARIAN VERSION OMIT BACON.

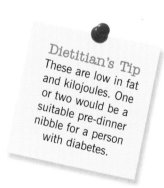

Dietitian's Tip

These are low in fat and kilojoules. One or two would be a suitable pre-dinner nibble for a person with diabetes.

Nutritional Information

PER MINI QUICHE		QUICHE	VEGETARIAN
FAT	TOTAL	2.8g	2.0g
	SATURATED	1.1g	0.8g
FIBRE		0.5g	0.5g
PROTEIN		4.2g	3.5g
CARBS		8.3g	8.2g
SUGAR		0.9g	0.9g
SODIUM		128mg	72mg
KILOJOULES		315(cals 75)	272(cals 65)
GI RATING		Medium	Medium

Mini Pizza Breads

MAKES: 40 SLICES

- ½ cup fresh tomatoes finely diced
- ¾ cup capsicum finely diced
- ½ cup shallots sliced or onion finely diced
- 1½ cups mushrooms finely diced
- ½ cup 97% lean ham (approx 4 slices) finely diced (Hans®)
- 1 cup 25% reduced fat grated tasty cheese
- 2 tablespoons grated parmesan cheese
- 1 teaspoon crushed garlic (in jar)
- ½ teaspoon dried oregano
- 1 large bread stick (340g)
- ⅓ cup no added salt tomato paste
- cooking spray

Dietitian's Tip

A low fat nutritious snack for your visitors who have diabetes

DIRECTIONS

Preheat oven 180°C fan forced. Place all the ingredients except bread and tomato paste into a large mixing bowl. Fold ingredients together well. Cut bread into 40 slices about 1 to 1½ cm thick. Spread a little tomato paste over each slice. Press approximately 1 tablespoon of mixture on top of each bread slice. Coat a large baking tray with cooking spray then place each pizza slice onto tray, bake 15-20 minutes or until cheese has melted and browned. Serve hot.

VARIATION: REPLACE HAM WITH ¾ CUP DICED CELERY FOR A VEGETARIAN VERSION.

Nutritional Information

PER SLICE		PIZZA	VEGETARIAN
FAT	TOTAL	1.1g	1.1g
	SATURATED	0.5g	0.5g
FIBRE		0.5g	0.5g
PROTEIN		2.1g	1.9g
CARBS		5.0g	5.0g
SUGAR		0.8g	0.8g
SODIUM		95mg	77mg
KILOJOULES		165(cals 39)	158(cals 38)
GI RATING		High	High

Salmon Mousse

SERVES: 20 AS AN APPETISER

- 250g low fat cottage cheese
- 1 x 415g can red salmon drained
- ⅓ cup shallots finely sliced
- 1 teaspoon wholegrain mustard (Masterfood®)
- 1 teaspoon lemon juice
- 2 tablespoons (30g) Flora Light® margarine
- 1½ tablespoons gelatine
- ¼ cup boiling water
- pepper to taste
- cooking spray

Dietitian's Tip

Low fat cottage cheese is also low in salt but high in protein. It is a great base for mousse and suitable for people with diabetes when combined with other healthy ingredients.

DIRECTIONS

Blend cottage cheese in food processor or blender until smooth. Add drained salmon and combine. Add shallots, mustard, lemon juice and margarine, blend well. Dissolve gelatine in boiled water, add to mixture. Blend until ingredients are well combined. Coat a small loaf tin with cooking spray then pour mixture into tin. Refrigerate until set. Turn out onto a serving plate (place the loaf tin in a little hot water for approximately 1 minute to allow the mousse to turn out easily). Serve with rice crackers, low fat Jatz or Cruskits cut in large squares, or sliced vegetables.

VARIATIONS: REPLACE WITH TUNA IN BRINE DRAINED, OR REPLACE LOAF TIN WITH EITHER A JELLY MOULD OR A ROUND CERAMIC BOWL DEPENDING ON SHAPE DESIRED.

Nutritional Information

PER SERVE		SALMON	TUNA
FAT	TOTAL	2.8g	1.4g
	SATURATED	0.6g	0.3g
FIBRE		0g	0g
PROTEIN		5.0g	5.5g
CARBS		0.4g	0.4g
SUGAR		0.4g	0.4g
SODIUM		137mg	101mg
KILOJOULES		197(cals 47)	152(cals 36)
GI RATING	*Not available due to the low carb content*		

Vegetable Samosas

MAKES: 40 SAMOSAS

1 cup cauliflower small florets

2 cups peeled potatoes diced

1 cup carrots diced

½ cup frozen peas

½ cup frozen corn kernels

cooking spray

½ cup onion diced

1 teaspoon crushed garlic (in jar)

1 teaspoon turmeric

1 teaspoon cumin

1 teaspoon dried coriander

¼ teaspoon dried chilli powder

1 teaspoon reduced salt vegetable stock powder (Massel®)

½ teaspoon salt

pepper to taste

10 sheets filo pastry (Antoniou®)

DIRECTIONS

To make filling: Microwave all vegetables in a little water for 12 minutes on HIGH. Drain, leave to one side. Generously coat a large non-stick frypan with cooking spray, sauté onion and garlic for 2 minutes. Add turmeric, cumin, coriander, chilli and stock powder to pan, mix well with onion. Fry 1 minute. Add vegetables, salt and pepper to pan. Gently stir ingredients until combined and cook for 3 minutes. Leave to cool. Preheat oven 200°C fan forced.

To make samosas: Using one filo sheet at a time, cut into 4 long strips. Spray pastry with cooking spray. Place a heaped dessertspoon of mixture onto top corner of one strip, fold mixture over to other side diagonally. Continue folding diagonally until you reach the end of the strip. Place samosa on a baking tray that has been coated with cooking spray. Repeat this method until 40 are made. Coat with cooking spray, bake 20-25 minutes or until lightly browned. Serve immediately as the pastry will soften when cooled. Serve with dipping sauces, sweet chilli, soy or tomato sauces.

Dietitian's Tip

These samosas are oven baked and not deep fried. This lowers the fat content making them lower in kilojoules and suitable for people with diabetes who are overweight.

Nutritional Information

PER SAMOSA

FAT TOTAL		0.2g
SATURATED		0g
FIBRE		1.0g
PROTEIN		1.4g
CARBS		4.6g
SUGAR		1.0g
SODIUM		47mg
KILOJOULES		109(cals 26)
GI RATING		High

Other Great Party Food Ideas

BOOK 1 - CORN CHIPS, MEXICAN MEATBALLS

BOOK 2 - SAUSAGE ROLLS

BOOK 3 - CHICKEN BITES, THAI FISH CAKES, MEXICAN DIP, CHEESE & SPINACH BREAD DIP, SPRING ROLLS

Desserts

Strawberry Custard Flan

SERVES: 10

BASE: 1 egg white

¼ cup sugar

3 tablespoons (45g) Flora Light® margarine melted

¼ cup skim milk

1½ cups self raising flour

cooking spray

CUSTARD: 1 x 375ml can evaporated light milk

3 tablespoons custard powder

3 tablespoons sugar

½ teaspoon vanilla essence

STRAWBERRY TOPPING: 1 packet strawberry diet jelly (Cottee's®)

½ cup boiling water

¾ cup cold water

1 x 250g punnet fresh strawberries

DIRECTIONS

Preheat oven 180°C fan forced.

To make base: In a medium sized mixing bowl beat egg white and sugar for 1 minute using an electric beater. Add margarine to milk, pour into egg mixture, combine. Add flour to bowl and fold together (don't overmix flour, as this will make the base tough). Coat a quiche dish with cooking spray, press base into dish using your hand (dip hand into flour so mixture doesn't stick). Press mixture out evenly over base and three quarters of the way up sides of the dish. Bake 15 minutes, leave to cool. **To make custard:** Place all custard ingredients into a medium sized saucepan, stir continuously using a whisk (don't have heat too high or milk will scorch). Once boiled, leave to cool slightly then pour over base. **To make topping:** Dissolve jelly crystals in a small bowl with boiling water then add cold water, stir well. Refrigerate mixture until jelly just starts to set (watch carefully as it takes anything from ¾ hour to 1 hour). Hull and wash strawberries. Cut in half and place decoratively over custard, forming a circle. Once jelly is almost set, spoon jelly over strawberries be careful not to let it run over the edge of dish. Refrigerate.

VARIATIONS:REPLACE STRAWBERRIES WITH ANY FRUIT OF YOUR CHOICE. MATCH UP COLOUR OF FRUIT WITH JELLY E.G. APRICOT HALVES AND ORANGE COLOURED JELLY.

Orange and Pineapple Whip

SERVES: 8

1 x 375ml can CHILLED evaporated light milk

1 x 440g can crushed pineapple unsweetened (Golden Circle®)

⅓ cup juice from canned pineapple

2 packets diet orange jelly (Cottee's®)

½ teaspoon imitation coconut essence (optional)

DIRECTIONS

Make sure evaporated milk is chilled before beginning. Drain pineapple, saving ⅓ cup of juice. Heat saved juice in microwave until near boiling. Dissolve jelly crystals in juice, leave to one side. In a large mixing bowl beat chilled milk and coconut essence using an electric beater until thick. Combine juice with drained pineapple then add to whipped milk, stir until combined. Refrigerate until set.

VARIATION: ADD ¼ CUP FRESH PASSIONFRUIT PULP TO MIX OR REPLACE ORANGE JELLY WITH ANY DIET JELLY OF YOUR CHOICE E.G. PINEAPPLE, PASSIONFRUIT OR LEMON.

Nutritional Information

PER SERVE		
FAT	TOTAL	3.1g
	SATURATED	0.9g
FIBRE		1.4g
PROTEIN		6.2g
CARBS		29.7g
SUGAR		12.9g
SODIUM		210mg
KILOJOULES		720(cals 171)
GI RATING		Medium

Nutritional Information

PER SERVE		
FAT	TOTAL	1.4g
	SATURATED	0.5g
FIBRE		0.6g
PROTEIN		5.1g
CARBS		10.8g
SUGAR		10.8g
SODIUM		62mg
KILOJOULES		291(cals 69)
GI RATING		Low

Chocolate Mousse Pie

SERVES: 12

**BASE: 12 low fat choc chip cookies
(Paradise Lite®)**
1 tablespoon (15g) Flora Light® margarine melted
¾ teaspoon skim milk
cooking spray
**FILLING: 24 squares (100g) dark cooking
chocolate**
1 x 375ml can CHILLED evaporated light milk
½ teaspoon vanilla essence
2 tablespoons gelatine
¼ cup boiling water
2 x Jarrah Choc-O-Lait® sachets

DIRECTIONS

Before starting make sure your evaporated milk is chilled. Place chilled canned milk into freezer for 1 hour before making filling. **To make base:** In a food processor crumble biscuits. Add melted margarine and milk, process until combined. Coat a pie plate with cooking spray then spread biscuit mixture over base, pressing firmly. Refrigerate. **To make filling:** In a small ceramic bowl melt chocolate in microwave on high temperature for one minute. Leave to sit in microwave while you prepare other ingredients. Make sure evaporated milk is very cold. In a large mixing bowl beat chilled milk and vanilla essence until really thick, using an electric beater. Add melted chocolate and blend well. Dissolve gelatine completely in boiling water then add Jarrah sachets, mix well. Pour mixture into milk, beat continuously until well combined. Pour mixture over biscuit base, refrigerate until set.

VARIATION: TO MAKE CHOCOLATE MOUSSE, OMIT BASE AND REDUCE GELATINE DOWN TO 1½ TABLESPOONS, SERVES 8.

Nutritional Information

PER SERVE	PIE	MOUSSE
FAT TOTAL	4.5g	4.4g
SATURATED	2.2g	2.7g
FIBRE	0.3g	0.2g
PROTEIN	5.6g	7.2g
CARBS	18.6g	15.0g
SUGAR	12.4g	12.9g
SODIUM	90mg	65mg
KILOJOULES	573(cals 136)	534(cals 127)
GI RATING	Low	Low

Coconut Cream Rice

SERVES: 6

1 litre skim milk
¼ cup sugar
¾ cup raw short grain rice
¼ teaspoon imitation coconut essence
1 tablespoon desiccated coconut

DIRECTIONS

Rinse starch off rice. Pour milk and sugar into a medium sized saucepan and bring to boil, stir occasionally. Keep on a medium heat so the milk doesn't burn on base. Add rice and once boiling, reduce to slow boil until rice is cooked (about 20 minutes). Stir frequently to avoid burning or sticking on base. Add coconut essence and coconut. Serve hot or cold. If mixture gets too thick add more skim milk. Serve on its own or with canned fruit in natural juice or stewed fruit.

VARIATION: FOR PLAIN CREAM RICE OMIT COCONUT ESSENCE AND COCONUT.

Dietitian's Tip

Again coconut essence is used to reduce the fat content and make it suitable for people with diabetes.

Nutritional Information

PER SERVE	COCONUT	PLAIN
FAT TOTAL	0.8g	0.3g
SATURATED	0.6g	0.2g
FIBRE	0.3g	0.2g
PROTEIN	7.9g	7.9g
CARBS	35.8g	35.7g
SUGAR	16.1g	16.0g
SODIUM	78mg	78mg
KILOJOULES	756(cals 180)	736(cals 175)
GI RATING	Medium	Medium

Berry Good Pudding

SERVES: 8

PUDDINGS: 2 egg whites

⅓ cup sugar

½ teaspoon bicarb soda

½ cup apple sauce (in jar)

¼ cup skim milk

1½ cups self raising flour

1 x 300g packet frozen raspberries, (reserving ¾ cup to be used for sauce)

SAUCE: ¼ cup sugar

1 cup water

¾ cup frozen raspberries (reserved from pudding ingredients)

Dietitian's Tip
The carbohydrate content is quite high but the dessert has a significant amount of fruit. Have one serve occasionally.

DIRECTIONS

Preheat oven 180ºC fan forced. **To make pudding:** In a medium sized mixing bowl beat egg whites and sugar for 1 minute, using an electric beater. Stir bicarb soda into apple sauce (it will froth) then add to bowl. Add milk and combine well. Gently fold sifted flour into mixture in one go, treat this mixture as if it is a sponge. DO NOT BEAT as this will make the pudding tough. Put aside ¾ cup of the frozen raspberries to be used for sauce below. Add remaining raspberries to pudding mix, gently fold through. Coat a 12 cup muffin tray with cooking spray then spoon an even amount of mixture into 8 muffin cups. Bake 20-25 minutes or until firm to touch in centre. **To make sauce:** In a small saucepan combine all sauce ingredients. Stir occasionally with a whisk until liquid boils. Reduce to a medium boil for 12 minutes. Place each pudding onto a dessert plate and pour an even amount of sauce over each one. Delicious served warm.

VARIATION: REPLACE WITH ANY FROZEN BERRIES.

Nutritional Information

PER SERVE		
FAT	TOTAL	0.5g
	SATURATED	0.1g
FIBRE		4.1g
PROTEIN		4.2g
CARBS		38.3g
SUGAR		19.7g
SODIUM		270mg
KILOJOULES		714(cals 170)
GI RATING		Medium

White Mud Cake with Blueberries

SERVES: 12

CAKE: 28 squares (110g) white chocolate

4 tablespoons (60g) Flora Light® margarine

1 cup sugar

¾ cup water

½ teaspoon bicarb soda

½ cup apple sauce (in jar)

2 egg whites

½ teaspoon vanilla essence

1¾ cups plain flour

¾ cup frozen blueberries

cooking spray

ICING: ¾ cup icing sugar

1 teaspoon (5g) Flora Light® margarine

a few drops vanilla essence

2 teaspoons skim milk

1 square white chocolate grated

Dietitian's Tip
Do not go back for seconds of this dessert as it is high in carbohydrates and kilojoules. This is definitely occasional food for a person with diabetes.

DIRECTIONS

Preheat oven 180ºC fan forced. **To make cake:** Place chocolate, margarine, sugar and water into a medium sized ceramic bowl. Microwave medium-low for 2 minutes. Stir ingredients then return to microwave for 1 minute. Stir until ingredients have dissolved. Mix bicarb soda into apple sauce (it will froth) then add to bowl. Whisk in egg whites and essence until combined. Sift flour into bowl then whisk ingredients until combined. Gently fold blueberries through mixture. Coat a 20cm round cake tin with cooking spray, then pour mixture into tin. Bake 50-55 minutes or until cake springs back when lightly pressed in centre. **To make icing:** In a small mixing bowl sift icing sugar. Add margarine and essence. Add enough milk to make spreadable then spread over cooled cake. Sprinkle grated chocolate over top to decorate.

VARIATIONS: REPLACE WITH FROZEN RASPBERRIES OR FROZEN MIXED BERRIES, OR OMIT BERRIES FOR A PLAIN WHITE MUDCAKE.

Nutritional Information

PER SERVE		
FAT	TOTAL	6.1g
	SATURATED	2.6g
FIBRE		1.1g
PROTEIN		3.6g
CARBS		45.3g
SUGAR		30.2
SODIUM		84mg
KILOJOULES		1026(cals 244)
GI RATING		Medium

Chocolate Self-Saucing Pudding

SERVES: 8

PUDDING: 2 egg whites

⅓ cup sugar

½ teaspoon bicarb soda

½ cup apple sauce (in jar)

¼ cup skim milk

1 cup self raising flour

¼ cup cocoa

SAUCE: ¼ cup cocoa

½ cup sugar

1¾ cups hot water

DIRECTIONS

Preheat oven 180ºC fan forced.

To make pudding: In a medium sized mixing bowl beat egg whites and sugar for 1 minute using an electric beater. Stir bicarb soda into apple sauce (it will froth) then add to bowl. Add milk and combine well. Sift flour and cocoa together. Gently fold flour into mixture in one go, treat this mixture as if it is a sponge. DO NOT BEAT as this will make the pudding tough. Coat a casserole dish (8 cup capacity) with cooking spray then pour mixture into dish. **To make sauce:** Sprinkle sifted cocoa and sugar over top of pudding then gently pour hot water over top. Bake 30-35 minutes or until firm to touch in centre.

> **Dietitian's Tip**
> This dessert is quite high in carbohydrate and will add little nutritional value to your eating plan. People with diabetes may like to calculate the amount of carbohydrate that they have eaten in their meal before adding this dessert. If you choose to eat this then do so only on special occasions.

Nutritional Information

PER SERVE		
FAT	TOTAL	1.0g
	SATURATED	0.5g
FIBRE		1.1g
PROTEIN		4.0g
CARBS		29.2g
SUGAR		15.5g
SODIUM		222mg
KILOJOULES		588(cals 140)
GI RATING		Medium

Lemon Tart

SERVES: 12

BASE: 15 low fat butternut cookies (Paradise Lite®)

1 teaspoon (5g) Flora Light® margarine melted

cooking spray

FILLING: 1 x 400g can condensed light milk

1 whole egg

½ cup skim milk

½ cup lemon juice

TOPPING: ¼ cup lemon juice

¼ cup sugar

2 tablespoons custard powder

½ cup water

> **Dietitian's Tip**
> A low fat dessert very high in carbohydrate and kilojoules. This is an occasional dessert.

DIRECTIONS

Preheat oven 180ºC fan forced. **To make base:** In a food processor crumble biscuits. Add melted margarine and process until combined. Coat a pie plate with cooking spray then spread biscuit mix over base, pressing firmly. Leave to one side. **To make filling:** In a medium sized mixing bowl blend condensed milk with whole egg and skim milk using an electric beater. Pour in lemon juice and combine well. Pour over base. Bake 20-25 minutes or until firm in centre. Leave to cool then make topping and pour over top. **To make topping:** Place all ingredients into a small saucepan, bring to boil, stir continuously. Sauce will thicken once boiled. Leave to cool slightly. Pour over top of baked tart.

Nutritional Information

PER SERVE		
FAT	TOTAL	1.6g
	SATURATED	0.7g
FIBRE		0.3g
PROTEIN		5.1g
CARBS		34.6g
SUGAR		29.6g
SODIUM		102mg
KILOJOULES		730(cals 174)
GI RATING		Medium

Fruit and Nut Cobbler

SERVES: 8

1 x 410g can peaches in natural juice drained

1 x 425g can pie apple unsweetened

1½ cups Special K® cereal

½ cup self raising flour

¼ cup pecan nuts chopped

¼ cup rolled oats

⅓ cup brown sugar

¼ teaspoon cinnamon

2 tablespoons (30g) Flora Light® margarine melted

1 teaspoon skim milk

Dietitian's Tip
Peaches and apples have a low glycemic index and are ideal for desserts for people with diabetes.

DIRECTIONS

Preheat oven 180°C fan forced. Place drained peaches in a casserole dish with pie apples and mix together. In a medium sized mixing bowl crush Special K using either potato masher or your fist. Add flour, pecan nuts, oats, sugar and cinnamon and combine well. Add melted margarine and milk, combine. Sprinkle over top of fruit. Bake 30 minutes or until browned.

VARIATIONS: REPLACE SUGGESTED FRUIT WITH ANY FRUIT OF YOUR CHOICE OR REPLACE SPECIAL K WITH BRAN FLAKES OR CORN FLAKES.

Hazelnut and Plum Flan

SERVES: 10

1 x 825g can plums in natural juice

2 egg whites

⅓ cup sugar

½ teaspoon bicarb soda

½ cup apple sauce (in jar)

½ cup ground hazelnuts

⅓ cup skim milk

1 cup cornflour (wheat-free)

cooking spray

Dietitian's Tip
Fruit in the flan increases the nutritional composition and makes this a healthy dessert.

DIRECTIONS

Preheat oven 180° fan forced. Drain plums then cut each plum in half, gently remove seeds. Leave to one side. In a medium sized mixing bowl beat egg whites and sugar for 1 minute using an electric beater. Stir bicarb soda into apple sauce (it will froth) then add to bowl. Add ground hazelnuts and milk and blend well. Gently fold sifted cornflour into mixture in one go, treat as if it is a sponge. DO NOT BEAT as this will make the flan tough. Coat a quiche dish with cooking spray then pour mixture into dish. Drop halved plums on top of mixture in a circle, cut side down. Bake 30-35 minutes or until firm to touch in centre. Serve hot or cold.

THIS IS IDEAL FOR ANYONE WHO HAS WHEAT INTOLERANCE, AS THE DISH IS WHEAT-FREE.

VARIATIONS: REPLACE PLUMS WITH ANY CANNED FRUIT HALVES IN NATURAL JUICE E.G. APRICOTS, PEARS OR PEACHES.

Nutritional Information

PER SERVE		
FAT	TOTAL	4.7g
	SATURATED	0.6g
FIBRE		2.2g
PROTEIN		3.3g
CARBS		28.3g
SUGAR		16.1g
SODIUM		124mg
KILOJOULES		697(cals 166)
GI RATING		Medium

Nutritional Information

PER SERVE		
FAT	TOTAL	2.8g
	SATURATED	0.1g
FIBRE		1.2g
PROTEIN		1.9g
CARBS		27.9g
SUGAR		16.1g
SODIUM		73mg
KILOJOULES		605(cals 144)
GI RATING		Low

Baking

Dietitian's Tip: The recipes featured in this section are good alternatives to traditional high fat baking, however it is important to look at your overall daily intake and try and keep 'extras' and excess kilojoules to a minimum if you wish to obtain good health. This section is high in kilojoules and should be chosen as a treat, not a daily occurrence. The best snack you can have is fruit but when a special occasion arises these recipes are ideal.

Chocolate Chip Cookies

SERVES: 24 COOKIES

1 egg white

½ cup sugar

4 tablespoons (60g) Flora Light® margarine

¼ cup skim milk

½ teaspoon vanilla essence

½ cup choc chips roughly chopped

1½ cups self raising flour

DIRECTION

Preheat oven 180°C fan forced. In a medium sized mixing bowl beat egg white and sugar for 1 minute using an electric beater. Melt margarine then add to milk, then add to bowl with vanilla essence and choc chips. Stir sifted flour into mix, combine well. Generously coat a baking tray with cooking spray then drop dessertspoons of mixture on tray, allowing for room to spread. Flatten each spoonful with the back of a fork that has been dipped in boiling water. Bake 20-25 minutes. Leave to cool on tray.

VARIATION: FOR DOUBLE CHOC CHIP COOKIES ADD ¼ CUP SIFTED COCOA IN WITH THE FLOUR.

Dietitian's Tip

Not much in the way of nutritional value but is low in fat and kilojoules. Can be included in the eating plan of a person with diabetes occasionally.

Marshmallow and Fruit Bubble Bar

SERVES: 20

1 tablespoon (15g) Flora Light® margarine

25 (125g) marshmallows (Pascal®)

¼ cup desiccated coconut

1 cup mixed dried fruit

4 cups Rice Bubbles® cereal

cooking spray

DIRECTIONS

Place margarine and marshmallows in a small ceramic bowl and microwave for 50 seconds on 50% power. Stir well until you have a smooth texture. If still lumpy put back in microwave for a further 30 seconds on 50% power. Fold coconut into marshmallow mix. Pour rice bubbles and dried fruit into a large mixing bowl, add marshmallow mix and combine well. Coat a slab tin with cooking spray then place mixture into tin. Use the back of a metal spoon that has been dipped in hot water to spread the mixture evenly. Refrigerate until set then cut into 20 slices.

Nutritional Information

PER COOKIE	CHOC	DOUBLE CHOC
FAT TOTAL	2.4g	2.5g
SATURATED	0.9g	1.0g
FIBRE	0.4g	0.4g
PROTEIN	1.3g	1.5g
CARBS	12.3g	12.5g
SUGAR	5.8g	5.8g
SODIUM	76mg	78mg
KILOJOULES	315(cals 75)	327(cals 78)
GI RATING	Medium	Medium

Nutritional Information

PER SERVE	
FAT TOTAL	1.2g
SATURATED	0.7g
FIBRE	0.8g
PROTEIN	0.8g
CARBS	15.7g
SUGAR	10.1g
SODIUM	67mg
KILOJOULES	299(cals 71)
GI RATING	High

Cheese and Onion Scones

MAKES: 12

2 tablespoons (30g) Flora Light® margarine

½ cup skim milk

2 egg whites

½ cup 25% reduced fat grated tasty cheese

1½ tablespoons grated parmesan cheese

⅓ cup shallots thinly sliced

2 cups self raising flour

cooking spray

extra ½ tablespoon grated parmesan cheese

> **Dietitian's Tip**
> A low fat savoury snack suitable for people with diabetes.

DIRECTIONS

Preheat oven 220°C fan forced.

Melt margarine in microwave, add to milk and combine. In a medium sized mixing bowl beat egg white with a fork until blended. Add grated cheese, 1½ tablespoons parmesan cheese and shallots, combine well. Sift flour into bowl in one go, fold together gently. Place dough onto a well-floured surface and roll out until about 1½ cm thick. Use either a 6cm scone cutter or glass that has been dipped into flour (to stop dough from sticking), cut out 12 scones. Coat a baking tray with cooking spray, place scones on tray so they are touching. Brush tops with a little milk. Sprinkle extra grated parmesan cheese over top of each scone. Bake 10-15 minutes. When cooked, either wrap in a tea towel or place on a wire rack to cool.

Nutritional Information

PER SCONE		
FAT	TOTAL	2.8g
	SATURATED	1.1g
FIBRE		0.9g
PROTEIN		4.9g
CARBS		17.7g
SUGAR		1.3g
SODIUM		232mg
KILOJOULES		487(cals 116)
GI RATING		Medium

Apricot and Honey Slice

MAKES: 15 SLICES

1 egg white

⅓ cup brown sugar

4 tablespoons (60g) Flora Light® margarine

3 tablespoons honey

2 tablespoons desiccated coconut

½ teaspoon cinnamon

¾ cup dried apricots chopped

⅓ cup rolled oats

3 cups Bran Flakes® cereal

¾ cup self raising flour

cooking spray

DIRECTIONS

Preheat oven 180°C fan forced. In a medium sized mixing bowl beat egg whites and sugar for 1 minute using an electric beater. Melt margarine then blend with honey, add to egg mix and combine. Add all other ingredients and fold together until flour has blended into mixture. Coat a slab tin with cooking spray then press mixture firmly into tin, use a metal spoon dipped in hot water to help flatten slice. Bake 20-25 minutes or until golden brown. Leave to cool then cut into 15 slices.

> **Dietitian's Tip**
> Dried apricots are high in vitamins and fibre and have a low glycemic index. It is good to incorporate them into a recipe suitable for people with diabetes.

VARIATIONS: REPLACE BRAN FLAKES WITH EITHER SPECIAL K OR CORN FLAKES, OR REPLACE DRIED APRICOTS WITH SULTANAS.

Nutritional Information

PER SLICE		
FAT	TOTAL	2.9g
	SATURATED	0.8g
FIBRE		2.4g
PROTEIN		2.3g
CARBS		21.2g
SUGAR		10.6g
SODIUM		142mg
KILOJOULES		498(cals 118)
GI RATING		Low

Iced Patty Cakes

MAKES: 12

PATTY CAKES

2 egg whites

¼ cup sugar

1½ tablespoons (25g) Flora Light® margarine

⅓ cup skim milk

½ teaspoon vanilla essence

1 cup self raising flour

12 paper patty cases

ICING

½ cup icing sugar

1 teaspoon (5g) Flora Light® margarine

approx 1 teaspoon skim milk

a few drops of food colouring

1 tablespoon sprinkles

Dietitian's Tip

Omitting the icing would make this suitable as an occasional snack for a person with diabetes. It contains refined foods of little nutritional value.

DIRECTIONS

Preheat oven 180°C fan forced. **To make patty cake:** In a medium sized mixing bowl beat egg whites and sugar for 1 minute using an electric beater. Melt margarine then add to milk and essence, pour into bowl. Gently fold sifted flour into mixture in one go, treat as if it is a sponge. DO NOT BEAT as this will make the cakes tough. In a 12 cup muffin pan place 12 paper patty cases. Spoon mixture evenly into cases. Bake 10 minutes or until firm to touch.

To make icing: Place icing sugar, margarine and a few drops of milk into a small bowl, stir together adding drops of milk until you have a spreadable consistency. Add a few drops of food colouring, mix in well. Spread icing over cooled patty cakes then top with sprinkles. Leave to set.

VARIATIONS: TO MAKE CREAM BUTTERFLY CAKES CUT OUT A SMALL HOLE IN CENTRE OF PATTY CAKES. SPOON ½ TEASPOON OF EITHER JAM OR LEMON SPREAD INTO CENTRE THEN TOP WITH MY SYMPLE SWEET CREAM (BOOK 3). MAKE ONLY ½ THE BATCH. CUT PIECE TAKEN FROM TOP AND SLICE IN HALF. PLACE ON TOP OF CREAM TO LOOK LIKE A BUTTERFLY, OR REPLACE JAM WITH COTTEE'S® DIET JAM FOR A LOWER SUGAR AND KILOJOULE COUNT, OR OMIT ICING FOR A PLAIN PATTY CAKE.

Nutritional Information

PER PATTY CAKE		ICED	JAM/CR	LEMON/CR	DIET JAM/CR	PLAIN
FAT	TOTAL	1.0g	1.0g	1.1g	1.0g	0.8g
	SATURATED	0.2g	0.3g	0.3g	0.3g	0.2g
FIBRE		0.4g	0.5g	0.5g	0.5g	0.4g
PROTEIN		2.0g	5.7g	5.7g	5.7g	2.0g
CARBS		18.9g	17.3g	16.6g	15.2g	12.2g
SUGAR		10.6g	9.1g	8.1g	6.9g	4.0g
SODIUM		100mg	125mg	125mg	127mg	98mg
KILOJOULES		381(cals 91)	419(cals 100)	413(cals 90)	386(cals 92)	266(cals 63)
GI RATING		Medium	Medium	Medium	Medium	Medium

Jam Drops

MAKES: 24

4 tablespoons (60g) Flora Light® margarine
3 egg whites
½ cup sugar
½ teaspoon vanilla essence
¾ cup cornflour
1 cup self raising flour
cooking spray
24 teaspoons berry jam

DIRECTIONS

Preheat oven 180ºC fan forced. Melt margarine, allow to cool slightly. In a medium sized mixing bowl beat egg whites until stiff and forming peaks using an electric beater. Like when making a meringue gradually add small amounts of sugar, beat well each time until sugar has dissolved. Add vanilla essence to margarine and pour into egg mix. Sift both flours then add to mixture in one go. Gently fold through until combined, treat this mixture as if it is a sponge. DO NOT BEAT as this will make the drops tough. Coat a flat baking tray with cooking spray, place dessertspoons of mixture onto tray, allowing for drops to spread. Using the back of a teaspoon that's been dipped in boiling water each time (shake off any water on spoon) make an indentation in centre of each drop. Place a teaspoonful of jam in centre. Bake 10-15 minutes or until firm to touch.

VARIATIONS: REPLACE WITH ANY JAM OF YOUR CHOICE, OR REPLACE JAM WITH LEMON SPREAD, OR LOWER THE SUGAR CONTENT REPLACE WITH COTTEES DIET JAM.

Nutritional Information

PER JAM DROP	JAM	DIET JAM	LEMON/SP
FAT TOTAL	1.3g	1.3g	1.5g
SATURATED	0.3g	0.3g	0.4g
FIBRE	0.3g	0.2g	0.2g
PROTEIN	1.0g	1.0g	1.0g
CARBS	15.8g	11.7g	14.5g
SUGAR	8.1g	3.8g	6.2g
SODIUM	58mg	60mg	62mg
KILOJOULES	327(cals 78)	259(cals 62)	316(cals 75)
GI RATING	Medium	Medium	Medium

Rich Chocolate Squares

MAKES: 15 SLICES

BASE: 2 egg whites
⅓ cup sugar
½ teaspoon bicarb soda
½ cup apple sauce (in jar)
⅓ cup cocoa
½ teaspoon vanilla essence
½ cup skim milk
½ cup Nutella® spread
1 cup self raising flour
cooking spray
ICING: 1 cup icing sugar
1½ tablespoons cocoa
2 tablespoons Nutella® spread
1–1½ tablespoons skim milk

Dietitian's Tip

Low in fat and moderate in carbohydrates. Do not go back for seconds. An occasional food for people with diabetes.

DIRECTIONS

Preheat oven 180ºC fan forced. **To make base:** In a medium sized mixing bowl beat egg white and sugar for 1 minute using an electric beater. Stir bicarb soda into apple sauce (it will froth) then add to bowl. Place sifted cocoa, vanilla essence, milk and Nutella into bowl and mix well. Gently fold sifted flour into mixture in one go, treat as if it is a sponge. DO NOT BEAT as this will make the slice tough. Coat a slab tin with cooking spray then pour mixture into tin. Bake 25-30 minutes or until firm to touch in centre. **To make icing:** Sift icing sugar and cocoa into a small mixing bowl. Place Nutella and milk into bowl, mix until a smooth icing is made. Add only enough milk to make the icing spreadable. Whilst slice is still warm spread icing over top, leave to cool. Once cooled, cut into 15 squares.

Nutritional Information

PER SLICE	
FAT TOTAL	3.8g
SATURATED	1.3g
FIBRE	0.8g
PROTEIN	3.1g
CARBS	30.0g
SUGAR	21.0g
SODIUM	143mg
KILOJOULES	682(cals 162)
GI RATING	Medium

Fruitastic Slice

SERVES: 15 SLICES

- 2 egg whites
- ¼ cup sugar
- ½ teaspoon bicarb soda
- ½ cup apple sauce (in jar)
- ½ cup dried dates chopped
- ½ cup dried apricots chopped
- ½ cup sultanas
- ½ cup currants
- ¾ cup peeled apple diced
- ½ teaspoon mixed spice
- ½ cup skim milk
- ¾ cup wholemeal self raising flour
- ¾ cup self raising flour
- cooking spray

Dietitian's Tip
This slice is full of nutritious fruit and is low in fat. Eaten in the amount recommended it can be taken between meals regularly by people with diabetes.

DIRECTIONS

Preheat oven 180° fan forced. In a medium sized mixing bowl beat egg whites and sugar for 1 minute using an electric beater. Stir bicarb soda into apple sauce (it will froth), add to bowl. Add all dried fruits, diced apple, mixed spice and milk. Sift both flours and gently fold into mixture in one go, treat as if it is a sponge. DO NOT BEAT as this will make the slice tough. Coat a slab tin with cooking spray then pour mixture into tin. Bake 25-30 minutes or until firm to touch. Allow to cool in tin then cut into 15 slices.

VARIATIONS: REPLACE ALL DRIED FRUIT (SULTANAS, CURRANTS, DATES, APRICOTS) WITH 2 CUPS FRUIT MEDLEY OR 2 CUPS MIXED DRIED FRUIT

Nutritional Information

PER SLICE	
FAT TOTAL	0.3g
SATURATED	0.1g
FIBRE	2.7g
PROTEIN	3.0g
CARBS	26.5g
SUGAR	17.2g
SODIUM	152mg
KILOJOULES	499(cals 119)
GI RATING	Low

Cherry Muffins

MAKES 10

- 1 x 55g Cherry Ripe® chocolate bar
- ¾ cup black cherries seedless drained (John West®)
- 2 egg whites
- ¼ cup sugar
- ½ teaspoon bicarb soda
- ½ cup apple sauce (in jar)
- ½ cup skim milk
- 1 teaspoon imitation coconut essence
- 2 cups self raising flour
- cooking spray

DIRECTIONS

Preheat oven 180ºC fan forced. Chop Cherry Ripe bar into small pieces. Cut cherries in half. Beat egg whites and sugar for 1 minute in a medium sized mixing bowl using an electric beater. Stir bicarb soda into apple sauce (it will froth) then add to bowl. Add chopped Cherry Ripe, cherries, milk and coconut essence, combine well. Gently fold sifted flour into mixture in one go, treat as if it is a sponge. DO NOT BEAT as this will make the muffins tough. Coat a 12 cup muffin tray with cooking spray then spoon mixture evenly into 10 muffin cups. Bake 20-25 minutes or until firm to touch in centre. Let sit in pan for 5 minutes then turn onto a cake rack.

VARIATION: TO MAKE CHOCOLATE CHERRY MUFFINS ADD ¼ CUP SIFTED COCOA.

Nutritional Information

PER MUFFIN	CHERRY	CHOC/CHERRY
FAT TOTAL	1.6g	1.9g
SATURATED	1.0g	1.2g
FIBRE	1.7g	1.9g
PROTEIN	4.3g	4.8g
CARBS	33.1g	33.6g
SUGAR	12.9g	12.9g
SODIUM	269mg	275mg
KILOJOULES	683(cals 163)	711(cals 169)
GI RATING	Medium	Medium

Ginger and Peach Loaf

SERVES: 10

½ cup boiling water

¾ cup dried peaches chopped

2 egg whites

¼ cup sugar

½ teaspoon bicarb soda

½ cup apple sauce (in jar)

¼ cup glacé ginger finely chopped

1 teaspoon ground ginger

1¾ cups self raising flour

cooking spray

DIRECTIONS

Preheat oven 180°C fan forced. In a small mixing bowl combine boiled water and dried peaches, leave to one side. In a large mixing bowl beat egg whites and sugar for 1 minute using an electric beater. Stir bicarb soda into apple sauce (it will froth) add to bowl. Place glacé ginger, ground ginger and peach mixture into bowl and combine. Gently fold sifted flour into mixture in one go, treat as if it is a sponge. DO NOT BEAT as this will make the loaf tough. Coat a loaf tin with cooking spray then pour mixture into tin. Bake 35 minutes or until firm to touch in centre. Allow loaf to sit for 5 minutes in tin before turning out onto a wire rack to cool.

Dietitian's Tip
This small amount of cake will provide you with enough carbohydrate for a snack. Make sure that you do not eat this too often and only have the serving size that is recommended.

Orange and Date Scones

MAKES: 12

2 tablespoons (30g) Flora Light® margarine

½ cup fresh orange juice

2 cups self raising flour

¾ cup dried dates chopped

2 tablespoons fresh orange peel grated

1 teaspoon sugar

2 egg whites

cooking spray

DIRECTIONS

Preheat oven 220°C fan forced. Melt margarine in microwave, add to juice and combine. Place sifted flour, dates, orange peel and sugar into a large mixing bowl. Using a fork beat egg whites with juice until combined. Pour into flour and fold together. Place dough onto a well-floured surface and press out with hands into a large round shape, about 1½cm thick (do not knead as it will make the scones tough). Use either a 6cm scone cutter or glass that has been dipped into flour (to stop dough from sticking), cut out 12 scones. Coat a baking tray with cooking spray, place scones on tray so they are touching. Brush tops with a little milk. Bake 10-15 minutes. When cooked either wrap hot scones in a tea towel or lift onto a cake rack to cool.

VARIATION: FOR A PLAIN DATE SCONE OMIT ORANGE JUICE AND PEEL, REPLACE WITH ½ CUP SKIM MILK.

Nutritional Information

PER SERVE		
FAT	TOTAL	0.4g
	SATURATED	0.1g
FIBRE		2.0g
PROTEIN		3.8g
CARBS		29.8g
SUGAR		12.2g
SODIUM		239mg
KILOJOULES		578(cals 138)
GI RATING		Low

Nutritional Information

PER SCONE		
FAT	TOTAL	1.5g
	SATURATED	0.3g
FIBRE		1.6g
PROTEIN		3.1g
CARBS		23.9g
SUGAR		7.4g
SODIUM		182mg
KILOJOULES		511(cals 122)
GI RATING		Medium

Orange and Pecan Teacake

SERVES: 10

CAKE
2 egg whites

¼ cup sugar

½ teaspoon bicarb soda

½ cup apple sauce (in jar)

½ cup sultanas

½ teaspoon cinnamon

½ cup fresh orange juice

2 tablespoons fresh orange peel grated

2 cups self raising flour

cooking spray

TOPPING
¾ teaspoon cinnamon

3 teaspoons sugar

¼ cup pecan nuts chopped

DIRECTIONS

Preheat oven 180° fan forced.

To make cake: In a medium sized mixing bowl beat egg whites and sugar for 1 minute using an electric beater. Stir bicarb soda into apple sauce (it will froth), then add to bowl. Add sultanas, cinnamon, orange juice and peel. Gently fold sifted flour into mixture in one go, treat this mixture as if it is a sponge. DO NOT BEAT as this will make the cake tough.Coat a 20cm round cake tin with cooking spray, then pour mixture into tin.

To make topping: Mix topping ingredients together and sprinkle over top of raw cake mix. Bake 35 minutes or until firm to touch in centre. Allow cake to sit for 5 minutes in tin before turning out. Carefully turn out onto a dinner plate then turn back onto a cake rack.

VARIATIONS: REPLACE PECAN NUTS WITH CHOPPED WALNUTS, OR OMIT PECANS FOR A LOWER FAT COUNT, OR REPLACE ORANGE JUICE AND RIND WITH LEMON JUICE AND LEMON RIND FOR A LEMON & PECAN TEACAKE.

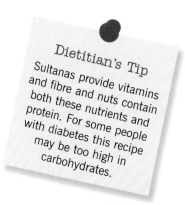

Dietitian's Tip
Sultanas provide vitamins and fibre and nuts contain both these nutrients and protein. For some people with diabetes this recipe may be too high in carbohydrates.

Nutritional Information

PER SERVE		PECAN	W/OUT PECAN
FAT	TOTAL	2.3g	0.5g
	SATURATED	0.2g	0.1g
FIBRE		1.9g	1.7g
PROTEIN		4.1g	3.9g
CARBS		35.8g	35.7g
SUGAR		15.7g	15.6g
SODIUM		264mg	264mg
KILOJOULES		748(cals 178)	676(cals 161)
GI RATING		Medium	Medium

Raspberry Coconut Slice

MAKES: 15 SLICES

BASE: 1 egg white

⅓ cup sugar

2 tablespoons (30g) Flora Light® margarine

¼ cup skim milk

1½ cups self raising flour

cooking spray

TOPPING: 1 cup raspberry jam

2 egg whites

⅓ cup sugar

¾ cup desiccated coconut

DIRECTIONS

Preheat oven 180°C fan forced. **To make base:** In a medium sized mixing bowl beat egg whites and sugar for 1 minute using an electric beater. Melt margarine then add to milk, pour into bowl and combine. Fold in sifted flour. Coat a slab tin with cooking spray then press mixture using your hand to flatten and spread evenly over tin (dip hand in flour so mixture doesn't stick). **To make topping:** Microwave jam for 30 seconds then spread evenly over base. In a medium sized mixing bowl beat egg whites until stiff and forming peaks using an electric beater. Gradually, like making a meringue add small amounts of sugar, beat well each time until sugar has dissolved. Fold coconut through then spread over jam. Bake 35-40 minutes. Leave to cool then cut into slices.

VARIATIONS: REPLACE JAM WITH ANY JAM , OR TO REDUCE THE SUGAR & KILOJOULES USE COTTEE'S® DIET JAM.

Symple Light Scones

MAKES: 12

2 egg whites

2 teaspoons sugar

2 tablespoons (30g) Flora Light® margarine

½ cup skim milk

2 cups self raising flour

cooking spray

Dietitian's Tip
Scones have little nutritional value. The only good thing is that they are often low in fat (total and saturated). The carbohydrate content is generally OK for one to be taken as a snack (17 to 20g).

DIRECTIONS

Preheat oven 220°C fan forced. In a medium sized mixing bowl beat egg whites and sugar together for 1 minute using an electric beater. Melt margarine in microwave, add to milk then pour into egg mix and combine. Sift flour into bowl in one go and fold together gently. Place dough onto a well-floured surface and press out with hands into a large round shape, about 1½ cm thick (do not knead as it will make the scones tough). Use either a 6cm scone cutter or glass that has been dipped into flour (to stop dough from sticking), cut out 12 scones. Coat a baking tray with cooking spray, place scones on tray so they are touching. Brush tops with a little milk. Bake 10-15 minutes. When cooked either wrap hot scones in a tea towel or lift onto a cake rack to cool.

VARIATIONS: FOR GINGER SCONES ADD 2 TEASPOONS GROUND GINGER AND ⅓ CUP GLACE GINGER (LOOSELY PACKED) FINELY DICED, OR FOR A FRUIT SCONE ADD ½ CUP OF EITHER SULTANAS OR CURRANTS.

Nutritional Information

PER SLICE	JAM	DIET JAM
FAT TOTAL	3.7g	3.7g
SATURATED	2.4g	2.4g
FIBRE	1.4g	1.1g
PROTEIN	2.5g	2.5g
CARBS	32.5g	19.4g
SUGAR	22.6g	8.8g
SODIUM	121mg	127mg
KILOJOULES	710(cals 169)	488(cals 116)
GI RATING	Medium	Medium

Nutritional Information

PER SCONE	PLAIN	GINGER	SULTANA	CURRANT
FAT TOTAL	1.5g	1.6g	1.6g	1.6g
SATURATED	0.3g	0.3g	0.3g	0.3g
FIBRE	0.9g	1.0g	1.2g	1.3g
PROTEIN	3.3g	3.3g	3.5g	3.4g
CARBS	17.6g	20.7g	23.6g	21.7g
SUGAR	1.2g	4.1g	7.0g	5.2g
SODIUM	185mg	186mg	188mg	188mg
KILOJOULES	410(cals 78)	464(cals 110)	513(cals 122)	481(cals 114)
GI RATING	Medium	Medium	Medium	Medium

Healthy Fruit Cake

SERVES: 12

1 cup dried mixed fruit

1 x 440g can fruit salad in natural juice (Golden Circle®)

¼ cup white sugar

1 teaspoon mixed spice

¼ cup water

1 cup All Bran® cereal

½ teaspoon bicarb soda

2 egg whites

1 cup self raising flour

cooking spray

Dietitian's Tip

This cake is full of nutritious fruit. The carbohydrate content may be too high for some people with diabetes.

DIRECTIONS

Preheat oven 180°C fan forced. In a medium sized saucepan place mixed fruit, whole can of fruit salad, sugar, mixed spice and water. Bring to boil then slow boil for 3 minutes. Pour mixture into a large mixing bowl then fold bran and bicarb soda into mix, leave to cool. Once cooled, stir in egg whites well then fold sifted flour through until combined. Coat a 19 cm cake tin or bar tin with cooking spray. Pour mixture into tin. Bake 30-35 minutes or until cake is firm to touch in centre.

VARIATIONS: REPLACE CANNED FRUIT SALAD WITH ANY OTHER CANNED FRUIT IN NATURAL JUICE OF YOUR CHOICE E.G. MANGO SLICES, CRUSHED PINEAPPLE.

Nutritional Information

PER SERVE		
FAT	TOTAL	0.6g
	SATURATED	0.1g
FIBRE		3.5g
PROTEIN		3.0g
CARBS		30.8g
SUGAR		20.8g
SODIUM		244mg
KILOJOULES		579(cals 138)
GI RATING		Low

Pineapple Upside Down Muffins

MAKES: 10

1 x 440g can pineapple slices in natural juice (Golden Circle®)

5 glacé cherries cut in half

cooking spray

10 teaspoons brown sugar

2 egg whites

¼ cup sugar

½ teaspoon bicarb soda

½ cup apple sauce (in jar)

2 cups self raising flour

Dietitian's Tip

Incorporating fruit into muffins increases the nutritional value. The high carbohydrate load of this recipe may make it unsuitable for many people with diabetes.

DIRECTIONS

Preheat oven 180°C fan forced. Drain pineapple rings, keep juice from the can to be used later. Slice 5 rings in half horizontally to form 10 thinner rings. Cut out a ¼ piece from each pineapple ring (so they will fit into muffin cup). Cut cherries in half. Coat muffin tray with cooking spray then sprinkle 1 teaspoon brown sugar into each muffin cup. Place pineapple ring over sugar, put cherry in centre of ring, repeat 9 times. Leave to one side. In a medium sized mixing bowl beat egg whites and sugar for 1 minute using an electric beater. Stir bicarb soda into apple sauce (it will froth) then add to bowl. Chop all remaining pineapple pieces from can, add to bowl with ⅓ cup of reserved juice. Gently fold sifted flour into mixture in one go, treat as if it is a sponge. DO NOT BEAT as this will make the muffins tough. Spoon mixture evenly into the 10 muffin cups. Bake 15-20 minutes or until firm to touch in centre. Let sit in pan for 5 minutes then turn out on a cake rack. Spoon any remaining syrup left in muffin cups over muffins.

Nutritional Information

PER MUFFIN		
FAT	TOTAL	0.4g
	SATURATED	0.1g
FIBRE		1.9g
PROTEIN		3.7g
CARBS		33.3g
SUGAR		13.5g
SODIUM		264mg
KILOJOULES		633(cals 151)
GI RATING		Medium

Master Index

Index

If you would like Annette to come and speak at your group, conference or seminar please phone:

The Symply Too Good To Be True Hotline (07) 5445 1250 (Int: +61 7 5445 1250)
Annette's Web Site - www.symplytoogood.com.au

Annette's cookbooks are sold in all good newsagents throughout Australia.

For information on stockists phone/fax the hotline or email: asym@bigpond.net.au

THREE EASY ORDER METHODS AVAILABLE
1. Website - secure online credit card orders, Austraila and international
2. Hotline - for credit card orders, Australia and international
3. Mail Order - Australia only. Download order form from website or ring the hotline or email for current price list. Send cheque or money order payable to: Annette Sym PO Box 833, Buddina, Qld 4575. Allow 7-21 days for delivery. Don't forget to include your mailing address.